# FINANCE FOR FARMING

# Finance for Farming

## A Guide for the Lending Banker

by
Keith Checkley

THE INSTITUTE OF BANKERS
10 Lombard Street, London EC3

First published: 1982
Reprinted 1983

ISBN: 0 85297 063 3 (paperback)

Printed and bound in England by Staples Printers Limited
at The Stanhope Press

*TO MY FAMILY AND FRIENDS*

# Foreword

The UK agricultural industry has an excellent record. Over the last 20 years it has shown a readiness to adopt, and adapt to, major technological changes that have resulted in substantial improvements in productivity and in the structure of the industry. UK farmers have been producing an increasing proportion of the nation's temperate-type food requirements – some 75% in 1981 compared with 63% in 1973.

While this may be good for the British economy, it has not all been easy going for most farmers. The rise in costs – farm inputs, running costs and the cost of capital items – has more than matched the higher output. So the financing of improved productivity, coupled with the cost/price squeeze, has inevitably called for increasing reliance by farmers on their bankers. For the first time, in May 1982, total borrowing from UK banks exceeded £4,000 million.

Over the years, The Institute of Bankers has been active in fostering an understanding of the special nature of farming finance, with lectures to its members around the country and an annual course on 'Agricultural Appreciation' for bankers. *Finance for Farming,* written by a banker whose day to day work involves him in the financial problems of his farming customers, is a most useful book which should help to promote an even better understanding of the needs of this very special industry.

*Richard Butler*

# Preface

Bank lending to farmers is very big business with £4 billion (£4,000 million) being lent to agriculture. At the end of 1981 the London Clearing Banks (the High Street banks) alone had some £2.7 billion of advances outstanding to farmers, more than one third of the total advanced to the whole of the manufacturing sector including the chemical industry, engineering, ship-building, vehicles, textiles, etc.

This substantial figure does not mean that the agricultural industry is in a parlous state. It has in fact a healthy balance sheet with borrowed funds representing only 11% of total assets, a low figure judged by normal commercial standards.

However, what may not be generally appreciated by many city folk is that the capital required to farm is staggering. As you may discover for yourself in the following pages, to buy the land and stock and equip a middle-of-the-road farm of say 300 acres would cost about £600,000. You could expect a return on capital of only about 3% although you would look hopefully for a steady increase in the value of your land.

Even a tenant farmer in this situation would require some £120,000 for working capital, stock and machinery. While he could expect a return of about 10%, there would be little compensation by way of capital appreciation.

In this book which has been written principally for banking students and bank managers 'at the sharp end' I have tried to give an overview of the farming industry with some specific comments on some basic farming enterprises. I have not attempted to deal with the more specialist activities such as poultry farming or fruit farming – or mushroom 'farming' (which properly belongs to a book on horticulture). However a major part of this book is devoted to *Farm Financial Planning* and *Assessing the Agricultural Lending Proposition*. The principles outlined in these chapters will apply to almost any undertaking where the value of stock-in-trade and the 'cash flow' of the business must relate to mother nature's cycle of production and reproduction and where the farmer, or grower, will need bank finance to tide him over the lean periods.

I have included, as appendices, some specimen forms used in farm financial planning and there is a glossary (Appendix 1) for readers unfamiliar with farming terminology.

I hope you will enjoy reading this book and that it will help you in your approach to the farmer.

## Acknowledgments

I am much indebted to the many organisations who have been most helpful in providing information, statistics, charts and specimen forms for the book: the Ministry of Agriculture, Fisheries and Food; The Agricultural Mortgage Corporation; the Agricultural Credit Corporation; the Central Council for Agricultural and Horticultural Co-operation; the Committee of London Clearing Bankers; the Information Office of the EEC; the Equipment Leasing Association; the Milk Marketing Board; the Meat and Livestock Commission; Wye College, University of London; Jones Lang Wootton (Chartered Surveyors); Thornton Barker (Chartered Accountants), and BASF UK (for the illustrations of crop diseases).

I also owe thanks to the following for looking at all, or parts of, the text: Bob Cooper of Highland Leasing; Phil Ethelston of Barclays Corporate Business Department and Philip Bolam of Barclays Group Agricultural Services Department.

I am especially grateful to Dr I. H. Rennie of ICI Farm Management Division; to The Institute of Bankers Chief Examiners in 'Practice of Banking', Bryan Hayter of Lloyds Bank and David Heard of Barclays Bank, who read and commented on the original text, and to the Institute staff who have been a source of encouragement and practical help throughout.

The book is based on my personal experience in dealing with farming customers. Any faults which remain are entirely my own.

*Keith Checkley, FIB*

# Contents

CHAPTER 1: **The UK Farming Scene**

An Overview . . . . . . . . . . . . . . . . . . . . . . . . . . . . . . . . . 1
Farm Types in Great Britain . . . . . . . . . . . . . . . . . . . . 3
Land Classifications . . . . . . . . . . . . . . . . . . . . . . . . . . . 3
'Agristats' . . . . . . . . . . . . . . . . . . . . . . . . . . . . . . . . . . . 5
Bank Lending Statistics . . . . . . . . . . . . . . . . . . . . . . . . 10

CHAPTER 2: **Farm Enterprises**

Dairy Production . . . . . . . . . . . . . . . . . . . . . . . . . . . . . 13
Beef Production . . . . . . . . . . . . . . . . . . . . . . . . . . . . . . 15
Sheep Production . . . . . . . . . . . . . . . . . . . . . . . . . . . . . 17
Pig Production . . . . . . . . . . . . . . . . . . . . . . . . . . . . . . . 18
Cereals . . . . . . . . . . . . . . . . . . . . . . . . . . . . . . . . . . . . . 21
Grassland Production . . . . . . . . . . . . . . . . . . . . . . . . . 22

CHAPTER 3: **Farm Financial Planning**

Gross Margin System . . . . . . . . . . . . . . . . . . . . . . . . . . 25
Gross Margin Budget . . . . . . . . . . . . . . . . . . . . . . . . . . 27
Farm Financial Planning . . . . . . . . . . . . . . . . . . . . . . . 28
Farm Budget for Profitability . . . . . . . . . . . . . . . . . . . 30
Net Worth Movement . . . . . . . . . . . . . . . . . . . . . . . . . 31
Farmer's Balance Sheet – Format . . . . . . . . . . . . . . . . 33

x

CHAPTER 4: **Assessing the Agricultural Lending Proposition**

Basic Points to Consider ........................ 37
Visiting the Farm .............................. 38
Financial Performance........................... 38
Looking at Asset Cover ......................... 38
Audited Accounts ............................ 38
The Farmer's Balance Sheet .................. 40
Example – Farmer A ............................ 41
Net Worth Trends............................ 44
Asset Structure.............................. 45
Gearing..................................... 45
Looking at 'Serviceability' ...................... 46
Rental Equivalent ........................... 47
Farm Budgets................................ 48
Example – Farmer B ............................ 51
– Farmer C .................... 57
Break-even Analysis ........................... 59
Cash Flow Forecasts .......................... 60
Looking at Security ........................... 64
Specimen Letter to Control .................... 65


CHAPTER 5: **Sources of Finance**

UK Farming Balance Sheet ..................... 67
Trade Credits................................. 68
Point of Sale Credit ........................... 68
Leasing ...................................... 69
Hire Purchase ................................ 70
Syndicate Credit.............................. 71
Insurance Companies ......................... 72
Private Loans................................. 72
Agricultural Credit Corporation .................. 72
Agricultural Mortgage Corporation .............. 74
Government Grants ........................... 77
Sale and Leaseback .......................... 78
Foreign Currency Loans ....................... 78
Return on Capital ............................ 79


CHAPTER 6: **Co-operatives in Agriculture**

Types of Co-operative ......................... 85
Financing of a Marketing Co-operative ........... 87
Summary on Co-operative Financing.............. 90
Example – Co-operative Society Budgets .......... 91

CHAPTER 7: **Taxation**

Income Tax . . . . . . . . . . . . . . . . . . . . . . . . . . . . . 99
Profit Averaging . . . . . . . . . . . . . . . . . . . . . . . . . . . 99
Stock Relief . . . . . . . . . . . . . . . . . . . . . . . . . . . . . 99
'Herd Basis' . . . . . . . . . . . . . . . . . . . . . . . . . . . . . 99
Capital Expenditure Allowances . . . . . . . . . . . . . . . 100
Capital Gains Tax . . . . . . . . . . . . . . . . . . . . . . . . . . 100
Capital Transfer Tax . . . . . . . . . . . . . . . . . . . . . . . 100

CHAPTER 8: **The European Economic Community**

Treaty of Rome – Member States . . . . . . . . . . . . . . . 103
EEC Institutions . . . . . . . . . . . . . . . . . . . . . . . . . . 104
Common Agricultural Policy (CAP) . . . . . . . . . . . . . 105
Finance . . . . . . . . . . . . . . . . . . . . . . . . . . . . . . . . 106
The Price Support System . . . . . . . . . . . . . . . . . . . . 109
The Future . . . . . . . . . . . . . . . . . . . . . . . . . . . . . . 109

APPENDICES:

1. Glossary of Farming Terms . . . . . . . . . . . . . . . 113
2. Metrication – Conversion Tables . . . . . . . . . . . . 116
3. Production Standards . . . . . . . . . . . . . . . . . . . 118
4. Checklist for Farm Visit . . . . . . . . . . . . . . . . . 121
5. Example – Farmer's Audited Accounts . . . . . . . . 123
6. Specimen Form – Bank's Review of Farming Customer's Account . . . . . . . . . . . . . . . . . . . . . . . 126
7. Example – Milk Marketing Board Forward Budget . . . . . . . . . . . . . . . . . . . . . . . . . . . . . 128
8. Example – ADAS Gross Margin Analysis . . . . . 129
9. Example – MLC Beefplan Report . . . . . . . . . . . 132
10. Checklist to Review Farm Business Finance . . . 134
11. Example – ADAS Development Plan . . . . . . . . . 136
12. Some Useful Addresses . . . . . . . . . . . . . . . . . . 140

INDEX                                                    141

CHAPTER 1

# The UK
# Farming Scene

## 1. AN OVERVIEW

I make no apology for this Chapter largely comprising a daunting array of figures which might otherwise have been relegated to an appendix. The Government's White Paper – *The Annual Review of Agriculture, 1982\** – contains many interesting statistics which I have restated, mainly under the heading 'Agristats'. The Chapter is by way of introduction to the farming scene, the extent of it and its significance in the UK economy.

The figures below are a modest sample of the wealth of information contained in the *Annual Review,* a publication which the lending banker should be well acquainted with. I would not suggest that you need to memorise the total amount of land given over to the production of various crops or the total numbers of various livestock in the country but the well-briefed banker should have some general appreciation of these economic indicators when talking to his farming customers.

On the other hand you will find it of practical value to compare the size of your own customer's farm enterprises and his production yields with the national averages, also to be familiar with land prices and average rents for tenant farmers.

(Here it is worth stressing that a farm enterprise is not synonymous with farm size. One farm may be engaged in a number of enterprises, e.g. dairy cows, sheep and crops, but the farm size and the type of land (see land gradings, below) will determine the nature and extent of the enterprises that can be profitably undertaken.)

The figures for *bank lending,* which I have also set out, clearly illustrate the increasing dependence on the farming community on financial assistance from the banks. As will be seen, the increase in bank lending over the last five years and month by month in the two years 1980 and 1981 has far outpaced the rate of inflation.

This is a summary of the main features:

*\*Annual Review of Agriculture* [Cmnd. 8491] HMSO, 1982.

*The farming industry's* contribution to Gross Domestic Product increased again in 1981 to *£4,493m* with 639,000 people employed in agriculture.

*The decline* in the number of farms continued with a total number of holdings of *242,300.* The formation of larger units continues to be the trend which has been seen over recent years.

*The total land usage* was 18·9m. hectares (or 46·7m. acres)† with 3·9m. hectares of land (9·6m. acres) down to cereals.

*Livestock numbers* continued to decrease with total animals at *131m.* The only sector which has increased is *sheep* – no doubt helped by the EEC Sheepmeat Regime which was introduced recently to support sheepmeat prices.

*Production yields* were slightly below the record level of 1980 but still represent significant growth over the last five years as a result of the improving technical performances of many farms.

*Bank borrowings* by the industry *increased by 20%* but this was a slowing down in demand compared with the previous four years. This is thought to link in with the lower levels of capital investment seen – total £915m. in 1981 as compared with £1,056m. in 1980.

*Farm incomes* showed some recovery in 1981 in most sectors but overall in the last six years *farm output* has risen by 59% with *farm costs* rising by 78% – hence the squeeze on farming margins.

*Land prices* have not shown the considerable rises which were seen in 1975–80. Prices in 1981 are broadly speaking at 1980 levels.

*1981*
Average price with vacant possession in:

|  | per hectare £ | (per acre) £ |
|---|---|---|
| England | 3,470 | (1,405) |
| Wales | 2,326 | (942) |
| Scotland | 1,830 | (740) |
| N. Ireland | 3,227 | (1,306) |

*Farm rents:* The rate of *increase* in rents fell to 14% in 1981 compared with 17% in 1980, the average rent being £63 per hectare (£26 per acre).

---

†One hectare = 2·47 acres. See the Imperial/Metric conversion table in Appendix 2.

## 2. FARM TYPES IN GREAT BRITAIN

The Ministry of Agriculture have classified farms into the following types:

Predominantly Dairying

Mainly Dairying

Livestock – Cattle

Livestock – Sheep

Pigs and Poultry

Cropping – Cereals

Cropping – General

Horticulture

Mixed

Looking at the chart (see centre pages) there is undoubtedly a pattern of *cropping in the East and dairying/livestock in the West*. This is due mainly to climatic; geological and topographical factors.

## 3. LAND CLASSIFICATION

Agricultural land is graded by the Ministry of Agriculture. The grades range from 1 to 5, according to the degree to which the land's physical characteristics will influence the agricultural use. (See soil classification chart on centre pages.)

### Description of the Grades

*Grade 1*

Land with very minor or no physical limitations to agricultural use. The soils are deep, well drained loams, sandy loams or peat, lying on level sites or gentle slopes and are easily cultivated. They retain good reserves of available water, either because of storage properties of the soil or because of the presence of a water table within reach of roots, and are either well supplied with plant nutrients or highly responsive to fertilisers. No climatic factor restricts their agricultural use to any major extent.

Yields are consistently high on these soils and cropping highly flexible since most crops can be grown, including the more exacting horticultural crops.

*Grade 2*

Land with some minor limitations which exclude it from Grade 1. Such limitations are frequently connected with the soil; for example, its texture, depth or drainage, though minor climatic or site restrictions, such as exposure or slope, may also cause land to be included in this grade.

These limitations may hinder cultivation or harvesting of crops, lead to lower yields or make the land less flexible than that in Grade 1. However, a wide range of agricultural and horticultural crops can usually be grown, though there may be restrictions in the range of horticultural crops and arable root crops on some types of land in this grade.

*Grade 3*

Land with moderate limitations due to the soil, relief or climate, or some combination of these factors which restrict the choice of crops, timing of cultivations, or level of yield. Soil defects may be of structure, texture, drainage, depth, stoniness or water holding capacity. Other defects, such as altitude, slope or rainfall, may also be limiting factors; for example, land over 122m. (400ft) which has more than 1015mm (40in) annual rainfall (1145mm (45in) ) in North West England, Western Wales and the West Country) or land with a high proportion of moderately steep slopes (1 in 8 to 1 in 5) will generally not be graded above 3).

The range of cropping is comparatively restricted on land in this grade. Only the less demanding horticultural crops can be grown and, towards the bottom of the grade, arable root crops are limited to forage crops (i.e. crops mainly for feeding animals). Grass and cereals are thus the principal crops; land in the middle range of the grade is capable of giving reasonable yields under average management. Some of the best quality permanent grassland may be placed in this grade where the physical characteristics of the land make arable cropping inadvisable.

*Grade 4*

Land with severe limitations due to adverse soil, relief or climate, or a combination of these. Adverse soil characteristics include unsuitable texture and structure, wetness, shallow depth, stoniness or low water capacity holding. Relief and climate restrictions may include steep slopes, short growing season, high rainfall or exposure. For example land over 183m (600ft) which has over 1270 (50in) annual rainfall or land with a high proportion of steep slopes (between 1 in 5 and 1 in 3) will generally not be graded above 4.

Land in this grade is generally only suitable for low output enterprises. A high proportion of it will be under grass, with occasional fields of oats, barley or forage crops.

*Grade 5*

Land with very severe limitations due to adverse soil, relief or climate, or a combination of these. The main limitations include very steep slopes, drainage, shallow depth of soil, excessive stoniness, low water holding capacity and severe plant nutrient deficiencies or toxicities. Land over 305m (1,000ft) which has more than 1525mm (60in) annual rainfall or land with a high proportion of very steep slopes (greater than 1 in 3) will generally not be graded above 5.

Grade 5 land is generally under grass or rough grazing, except for occasional pioneer forage crops.

From the chart it can be seen that most land is classified Grade 3 and the best land (Grades 1 and 2) is found mainly in the Eastern counties.

More detailed maps of land classification on a county basis can be obtained from the Ministry of Agriculture.

*Note.* Land grading has recently been changed to:

|      | 1A | 1B | 1C | 2 | and | 3 | *New Grades* |
|------|----|----|----|---|-----|---|--------------|
| from | 1  | 2  | 3  | 4 |     | 5 | *Old Grades* |

## 4. 'AGRISTATS'

(Data Source – Annual Review of Agriculture 1982.)

### i. Agriculture in the national economy

Agriculture is one of the largest industries, with a contribution, in 1981, of £4,493m to the gross domestic product.

**Contribution to Gross Domestic Product**

|  | 1976 | 1977 | 1978 | 1979 | 1980 | 1981 |
|---|---|---|---|---|---|---|
| £m | 2,947 | 3,154 | 3,415 | 3,728 | 4,102 | 4,493 |
| Percentage: | 2·7% | 2·5% | 2·4% | 2·3% | 2·1% | 2·1% (estimated) |

The number of people employed in 1981 in agriculture was 639,000 and represents 2·8% of total manpower engaged in all occupations. The workforce is declining: it averaged 753,000 over the years 1969–1971.

Although the area of land farmed is also declining, the degree of self-sufficiency in food in the United Kingdom has increased.

**Value of home-produced food as a percentage of indigenous type food consumed in the United Kingdom**

| 1976 | 1977 | 1978 | 1979 | 1980 | 1981 |
|---|---|---|---|---|---|
| 68·4% | 66·9% | 70·2% | 71·4% | 75% | 75% (estimated) |

### ii. Land Usage
(1 Hectare=2·47 Acres)

**Crop Areas ('000 hectares)**

| 1976 | 1977 | 1978 | 1979 | 1980 | 1981 |
|---|---|---|---|---|---|
| 19,094 | 18,948 | 18,953 | 18,936 | 18,931 | 18,908 |

|  | 1980 | 1981 | 1980 | 1981 |
|---|---|---|---|---|
|  | Area ('000 hectares) | | % Total Area | |
| Wheat | 1,441 | 1,493 | 7·6 | 7·9 |
| Barley | 2,338 | 2,338 | 12·3 | 12·3 |
| Oats | 148 | 142 | 0·8 | 0·8 |
| Other grain | 19 | 17 | 0·1 | 0·1 |
| Total cereals | 3,946 | 3,990 | 20·8 | 21·1 |
| Potatoes | 205 | 190 | 1·1 | 1·0 |
| Sugar beet | 213 | 210 | 1·1 | 1·1 |
| Oilseed rape | 93 | 125 | 0·5 | 0·6 |
| Horticulture | 274 | 253 | 1·4 | 1·3 |
| Other crops & fallow | 305 | 316 | 1·6 | 1·6 |
| Total tillage | 5,036 | 5,084 | 26·5 | 26·7 |

|                                            | 1980 | 1981 | 1980 | 1981 |
|--------------------------------------------|------|------|------|------|
|                                            | *Area ('000 hectares)* | | *% Total Area* | |
| Temporary grass (Under 5 years old)        | 1,982 | 1,915 | 10·5 | 10·2 |
| Total arable                               | 7,018 | 6,999 | 37·0 | 36·9 |
| Permanent grass (5 years old and over)     | 5,132 | 5,111 | 27·1 | 27·0 |
| Rough grazing                              | 6,293 | 6,312 | 33·3 | 33·5 |
| Other land                                 | 488 | 486 | 2·6 | 2·6 |
|                                            | 18,931 | 18,908 | 100% | 100% |

Hence the total arable acreage is 37% showing the large area of land still devoted to livestock farming.

Also interesting to note is the small area (1·3%) devoted to horticulture, although this is a sector of very high output per hectare.

### iii. Livestock Numbers*

|                              | 1980 | 1981 |
|------------------------------|------|------|
|                              | *('000 head)* | |
| Dairy cows                   | 3,226 | 3,212 |
| Beef cows                    | 1,488 | 1,428 |
| Heifers in calf              | 839 | 869 |
| Other cattle & calves        | 7,918 | 7,700 |
| Total cattle & calves        | 13,471 | 13,209 |
| Ewes                         | 12,149 | 12,561 |
| Shearlings                   | 2,735 | 2,773 |
| Other sheep & lambs          | 16,508 | 16,748 |
| Total sheep & lambs          | 31,392 | 32,282 |
| Sows for breedings           | 721 | 730 |
| Gilts in pig                 | 110 | 111 |
| Other pigs                   | 7,026 | 7,012 |
| Total pigs                   | 7,857 | 7,853 |
| Table fowls (inc. broilers)  | 61,528 | 59,043 |
| Laying fowls                 | 46,762 | 44,519 |
| Growing pullets              | 15,109 | 12,975 |
| Other poultry                | 14,481 | 14,250 |
| Total poultry                | 137,870 | 130,797 |

*For readers unfamiliar with farming terminology for livestock at various stages of development there is a glossary on page 113.

All sectors have decreased over the past five years *with the exception of sheep* where we have seen a gradual increase in numbers – no doubt helped by the introduction of the EEC Sheepmeat Regime.

## iv. Production Yields

### Estimated average yields of crops and livestock products

| | 1976 | | 1981 | |
| | tonnes per hectare | (tons per acre) | tonnes per hectare | (tons per acre) |
|---|---|---|---|---|
| Wheat | 3·85 | (1·53) | 5·63 | (2·24) |
| Barley | 3·51 | (1·39) | 4·41 | (1·76) |
| Oats | 3·25 | (1·29) | 4·48 | (1·78) |
| Potatoes | 21·60 | (8·59) | 31·03 | (12·56) |
| Sugar (in-beet) | 4·20 | (1·67) | 5·90 | (2·35) |
| Oil seed rape | 2·30 | (0·91) | 2·60 | (1·04) |
| Apples: | | | | |
|   Dessert | 10·82 | (4·30) | 8·66 | (3·45) |
|   Culinary | 11·59 | (4·61) | 8·25 | (3·29) |
| Pears | 13·16 | (5·24) | 9·87 | (3·93) |
| Tomatoes | 137·30 | (54·65) | 148·67 | (59·23) |
| Cauliflowers | 16·50 | (6·57) | 19·35 | (7·71) |
| Hops | 1·35 | (0·54) | 1·66 | (0·66) |

*Livestock products* (366 days)

| | Litres/ Cow | (Gallons/ Cow) | Litres/ Cow | (Gallons/ Cow) |
|---|---|---|---|---|
| Milk | 4,264 | (938) | 4,710 | (1,036) |
| Eggs (Number per bird) | 238·5 | | 251·5 | |

The increased yields over the past five years are significant and relate to the improving technical performances of many farms. (Apples and pear yields were *down* in 1981 owing to widespread poor cropping conditions.)

## v. Size of Business

Standard man-days are frequently used for farm size and farm type classification (1 S.M.D.=8 labour hours).

### Number of holdings ('000)

| | 1976 | 1981 |
|---|---|---|
| under 250 s.m.d. (per annum) | 126·2 | 122·4 |
| 250 to 499 s.m.d. | 56·4 | 46·4 |
| 500 to 999 s.m.d. | 45·8 | 43·6 |
| 1,000 s.m.d. and over | 28·3 | 29·9 |
| Total | 256·8 | 243·3 |

This shows not only a *decrease* in the total number of agricultural holdings but a definite trend to larger units in the 1,000 s.m.d. and over sector. This trend is confirmed when you look at the average size of enterprises.

**Average size of enterprises***

| | 1976 | | 1981 | |
|---|---|---|---|---|
| | *Hectares* | *(Acres)* | *Hectares* | *(Acres)* |
| Crops and grass | 47·2 | (117) | 50·7 | (125) |
| Cereals | 30·5 | (75) | 38·3 | (95) |
| Potatoes | 3·7 | (9·1) | 4·3 | (10·6) |
| Sugar beet | 15·4 | (38·1) | 12·8 | (31·6) |

**Numbers per enterprise**

| | 1976 | 1981 |
|---|---|---|
| Dairy cows | 40 | 53 |
| Beef cows | 19 | 18 |
| Breeding sheep | 168 | 184 |
| Breeding pigs | 23 | 37 |
| Fattening pigs | 161 | 241 |
| Laying fowls | 611 | 762 |
| Broilers | 23,927 | 27,350 |

## vi. Capital Investment

With the decrease in labour force; formation of larger farming units and improved technical farming performances, we have seen an increase over the years in capital investment in buildings, plant and machinery. However, more recently there is evidence of a definite cut-back in *machinery* investment (1980 and 1981), and in *machinery* and *buildings* in 1981.

| £m at current prices | 1976 | 1977 | 1978 | 1979 | 1980 | 1981 |
|---|---|---|---|---|---|---|
| Plant, machinery and vehicles | 438 | 514 | 582 | 629 | 547 | 440 |
| Building and works | 225 | 249 | 332 | 389 | 509 | 475 |
| Total | 663 | 762 | 915 | 1,018 | 1,056 | 915 |

## vii. Output, Costs and Income

| £m | 1976 | 1977 | 1978 | 1979 | 1980 | 1981 |
|---|---|---|---|---|---|---|
| Gross output | 6,133 | 6,892 | 7,298 | 8,163 | 8,886 | 9,733 |
| *less* costs | 4,850 | 5,636 | 6,055 | 7,018 | 7,861 | 8,524 |
| Farming income | 1,283 | 1,256 | 1,243 | 1,145 | 1,025 | 1,209 |

The table shows how the substantial increase in production (59%) over the years has been outpaced by the increase in farming costs (78%). This clearly indicates the

*N.B. Not to be confused with farm size. A single farm business may be involved in a number of different enterprises.

resulting squeeze on margins experienced in farming over the past few years, although in 1981 the decline in farming income was halted.

The following survey of net incomes for different types of farm (in England) illustrates the trend:

| Type of farm | Average net income per farm for an identical sample | | |
|---|---|---|---|
| | 1979 | 1980 | 1981 |
| *England* | £ | £ | £ |
| Specialist dairy | 8,013 | 6,334 | 7,707 |
| Mainly dairy | 11,172 | 8,343 | 9,760 |
| Cattle and Sheep | | | |
| Hill | 9,205 | 4,195 | 6,117 |
| Lowland | 3,098 | 1,176 | 2,069 |
| Crops/cattle and sheep | 7,426 | 4,882 | 4,042 |
| Specialist cereals | 9,295 | 7,397 | 9,162 |
| General cropping | 12,685 | 13,830 | 10,168 |
| Pigs and poultry | 13,215 | 10,795 | 12,655 |

This survey shows the widespread falls in income in 1980 with some recovery in 1981. The return that this income represents on capital employed in farming is discussed in Chapter 5.

## viii. Land Tenure, Prices and Rents

The proportion of the total area held by owner-occupiers has increased from 52% in 1960 to 59% in 1981.

Land prices have risen steadily through that period although they have fallen back recently, broadly speaking to 1980 levels.

**Agricultural Land Prices**

*£ per hectare (£ per acre)*

| | 1978 | 1979 | 1980 | 1981 |
|---|---|---|---|---|
| *England* | | | | |
| With vacant | | | | |
| possession | 1,994 (807) | 2,602 (1,053) | 3,227 (1,306) | 3,470 (1,405) |
| Tenanted | 1,563 (632) | 1,687 (683) | 2,281 (968) | 2,336 (946) |
| *Wales* | | | | |
| With vacant | | | | |
| possession | 1,327 (537) | 1,788 (724) | 2,482 (1,005) | 2,326 (942) |
| Tenanted | 628 (254) | 818 (331) | 1,064 (430) | 1,188 (481) |
| *Scotland* | | | | |
| With vacant | | | | |
| possesion | 1,062 (430) | 1,085 (439) | 2,057 (833) | 1,830 (741) |
| Tenanted | 632 (256) | 694 (280) | 1,167 (472) | 1,552 (628) |
| *N. Ireland* | | | | |
| With vacant | | | | |
| possession | 1,846 (747) | 2,618 (1,060) | 3,327 (1,347) | 3,227 (1,306) |

(*Note:* Very little land is rented in Northern Ireland.)

**Rents**

*Average rent per hectare (per acre)*

| Region | £ | £ | Region | £ | £ |
|--------|---|---|--------|---|---|
| Eastern | 77·5 | (31·3) | Yorks. & Lancs. | 54·5 | (22·1) |
| S.E. | 76 | (30·7) | Northern | 38 | (15·3) |
| E. Midlands | 75·5 | (30·6) | Wales | 32 | (13) |
| W. Midlands | 67 | (27) | England | 63·5 | (25·7) |
| S. Western | 62 | (25·1) | England & Wales | 60·5 | (24·4) |

Rents have increased at an average of 16% per annum over the last three years. (Average rents for Scotland are not published as there are wide variations between types of land.)

## 5. BANK LENDING STATISTICS

### TABLE 1

**All Banks Advances to Agriculture, Forestry and Fishing**

|      |          | £m     |
|------|----------|--------|
| 1980 | May      | £2,752 |
|      | August   | £3,039 |
|      | November | £3,075 |
| 1981 | February | £3,099 |
|      | May      | £3,345 |
|      | August   | £3,585 |
|      | November | £3,560 |

**London Clearing Banks Advances to Agriculture, Forestry and Fishing**

|      |          |        |
|------|----------|--------|
| 1980 | May      | £1,992 |
|      | August   | £2,207 |
|      | November | £2,247 |
| 1981 | February | £2,244 |
|      | May      | £2,466 |
|      | August   | £2,641 |
|      | November | £2,664 |

(At the end of 1981, total bank lending included £85m. to the fishing industry, of which £35m. was from the London Clearing Banks. A separate figure for forestry is not published.)

## TABLE 2
### London Clearing Banks Advances to Agriculture
### (August Annually)

|      | £m    | Percentage increase on previous year |
|------|-------|--------------------------------------|
| 1976 | 811   | —                                    |
| 1977 | 1,026 | + 27                                 |
| 1978 | 1,318 | + 28                                 |
| 1979 | 1,738 | + 32                                 |
| 1980 | 2,205 | + 27                                 |
| 1981 | 2,641 | + 20                                 |

## TABLE 3 (A)
### London Clearing Banks Advances to Agriculture on a Monthly Basis

|           | £m 1979 | 1980  | Percentage increase |
|-----------|---------|-------|---------------------|
| January   | 1,453   | 1,928 | 33                  |
| February  | 1,393   | 1,857 | 33                  |
| March     | 1,380   | 1,857 | 35                  |
| April     | 1,490   | 1,982 | 33                  |
| May       | 1,538   | 1,989 | 29                  |
| June      | 1,585   | 2,098 | 32                  |
| July      | 1,655   | 2,215 | 34                  |
| August    | 1,738   | 2,205 | 27*                 |
| September | 1,752   | 2,228 | 27*                 |
| October   | 1,817   | 2,302 | 27*                 |
| November  | 1,791   | 2,246 | 25*                 |
| December  | 1,854   | 2,284 | 23*                 |

*Slowing down in demand.

## TABLE 3 (B)
### London Clearing Banks Advances to Agriculture on a Monthly Basis

|           | £m 1980 | 1981  | Percentage increase |
|-----------|---------|-------|---------------------|
| January   | 1,928   | 2,255 | 17                  |
| February  | 1,857   | 2,243 | 21                  |
| March     | 1,857   | 2,243 | 21                  |
| April     | 1,982   | 2,430 | 23                  |
| May       | 1,989   | 2,463 | 24                  |
| June      | 2,098   | 2,522 | 20                  |
| July      | 2,215   | 2,644 | 19                  |
| August    | 2,205   | 2,641 | 20                  |
| September | 2,228   | 2,683 | 20                  |
| October   | 2,302   | 2,617 | 14                  |
| November  | 2,246   | 2,664 | 19                  |
| December  | 2,284   | 2,686 | 18                  |

**In conclusion**

I hope from the data you have seen it will be appreciated that agriculture is an important sector of bank lending to a large complex and demanding industry.

Agricultural measurement at the moment is an unsatisfactory mixture of the *Imperial* and *Metric* systems. It is confusing to all. You will often find farmers talking in acres of land farmed, and at the same time litres of milk yielded. I apologise if I fall into the same trap in the following chapters. Remember 1 Hectare = 2·47 Acres. (A conversion table for Imperial/Metric measurements is given in Appendix 2.)

In Chapter 2 we look at the farm enterprises you are most likely to encounter when visiting the farm.

CHAPTER 2

# Farm Enterprises

A lot of bank managers I know are uncomfortable when 'walking the farm' as they feel unsure of the basic factors involved in farming. I hope the following brief comments in this Chapter will help. Although it would be possible to write a Chapter on each farm enterprise, I have attempted to summarise the main points on some of the most commonly found enterprises. For readers unfamiliar with farming terminology there is a glossary on page 113.

## 1. DAIRY PRODUCTION

The *Friesian* breed (which originated in the Netherlands) dominates the scene as a 'high yielding' cow.

The target liveweight of a cow (heifer) when it produces its first calf is 500 kgs at between 2 and 2½ years of age. A mature Friesian cow will weigh 600 kgs.

In a self-contained dairy herd the farmer will rear his own dairy replacements and will aim for a target of 20% replacement rate per annum. (The national average is around 25%.)

### Milk

In theory, a cow will be in milk 305 days and dry 60 days. The *gestation period is 9 months*. The milk yield increases to a peak 6/8 weeks after calving and then falls off at approx. 10% per month. (See lactation curve on page 14.)

The maximum daily yield will be approx. 1/200 of the total: e.g. say 27 litres × 200 = 5455 litres (total over 10 months).

The fundamentals for dairy production remain unchanged: feed well; increase the animals' body weight before calving to give a high peak yield (known as 'steaming-up'); look after the animals and use a good milking technique – dairy cows are sensitive creatures!

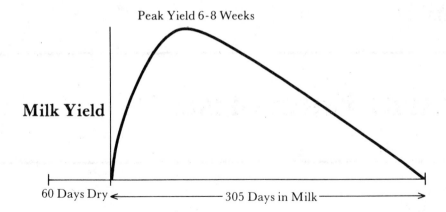

Cow accommodation is therefore very important and cow grouping into high yielders, low yielders and dry cows will help with feeding management.

You will hear some farmers talking of milking their cows *three* times a day as the cow's milk cells in the udder will be stimulated to produce up to 25% more milk! However, against this must be offset the extra labour, fuel and machinery costs. Also the extra milk tends only to be produced in the first 100 days of lactation (although there is recent evidence that increased milk yield can carry on right through lactation to give an increased yield of 18% approximately).

### Cow Diet

Dairy cows have tremendous appetites and feed bills can amount to 45/50% of the value of the milk sales! Therefore it is very important to make the best use of the cheapest food – grass. For grass production there is a saying 'West is best' (because of its generally more favourable climate).

The following illustrates the dietary value of grass compared with silage. Grass provides maintenance (basic sustenance of the cow) plus 23 litres of milk production per day compared with 4·5 litres for silage.

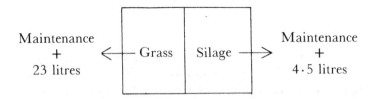

Making silage for winter feed is important for *quality* as well as *quantity*. Some farmers are better at this than others and will produce silage of M + 9/14 litres. The balance will need to be made up of concentrates bought at an average price of £130 per ton.

The quantity of silage needed for winter feed will depend on the locality of the farm and the length of period required for winter housing. A figure to remember is 6/9t. silage per cow per winter.

## Stocking Rate

This is again an important area. The farmer must use his land effectively.
   A general guide to stocking rates is:

   1 cow to 1·7 acres – LOW
   1 cow to 1·4 acres – AVERAGE
   1 cow to 1·2 acres – FAIRLY HIGH
   1 cow to 1    acre  – HIGH

## 'Flying Herd'

This graphic description applies to the situation where the farmer does not rear his
own dairy herd replacements. Cows are culled out (i.e. sold for slaughter) when
past their best and replacements purchased as necessary.
The main disadvantage is not always knowing the pedigree of the replacement cows
being purchased. There are, however, cost-saving advantages and land can be freed
for alternative use.

## Enterprise Monitoring

Most farmers will participate in some form of enterprise monitoring scheme. Bank
managers can get useful comparative information from this source, both of a financial
and technical nature (see later, in Chapter 4).

### Summary of Main Economic Factors in Dairy Production
   i  Milk yield – summer or winter predominance will affect price.
   ii  Concentrate costs.
   iii  Stocking rates (grazing costs).
   iv  Cost of replacement animals.

   It is worth remembering that, whilst the dairy enterprise is often the one that
produces the highest and most regular income (monthly milk cheques), it can also
be responsible for devouring large chunks of capital!

## 2. BEEF PRODUCTION

Most beef production originates from the Dairy-Herd. Almost 75% of beef in the
UK comes from the fattening of cross-bred calves out of Friesian dairy cows. Other
production comes from beef herds – either single suckled or multiple suckled (see
below). A small percentage of beef production comes from the cull-cow trade (dairy
cows past their best).
   Hexham livestock market was my earliest impression of an active livestock market.
I can recall at the age of about eight watching the 'wheeling and dealing' of the
astute livestock men. Profitability in beef can be so dependent on buying and selling
right!
   The farmer in selecting the 'beef' bull will want to consider the rate of liveweight

gain and also the pedigree of the bull. Records can usually be obtained through the Milk Marketing Board, who can supply lists of 'nominated' bulls.

The following simple chart illustrates the comparative speed of liveweight gain of the three main breeds in the UK.

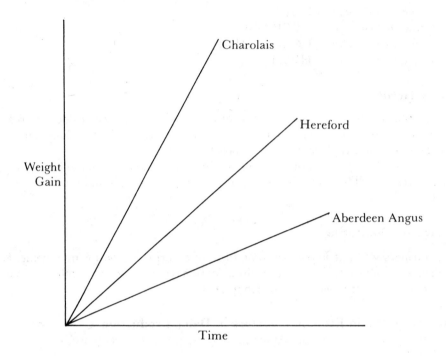

The Charolais and Aberdeen Angus produce large and small calves respectively; whilst the Hereford tends to be the middle-of-the-road breed which has proved to be the most popular as a crossbreed calf producer.

## Diet
The time-scale for beef production (12, 18 or 24 months) depends on the selection of animal feed. It should be remembered that the two cheapest sources of feed are grass and home-produced barley.

### 12 Month or 'Barley' Beef
This is a method of intensive beef production intended to achieve a liveweight of 400 kgs. without any grazing at all. A good food conversion rate is essential to produce the target weight as quickly as possible.

Faster growth can be achieved by rearing 'entires' (uncastrated bulls) but there are safety controls to be observed (bulls are not the most docile of animals) as well as problems in locating a suitable slaughter-house.

The following illustrates the relative speed of weight gain:

*entire* – 1.25 kgs. weight gain per day.
*castrate* – 1.05 kgs. weight gain per day.

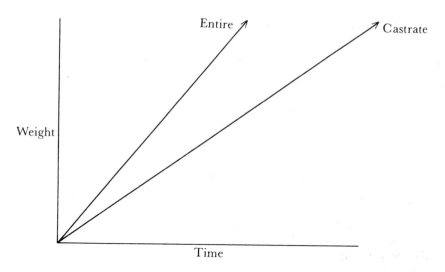

*18 month semi-intensive beef*
This calls for fattening on a mixture of grazing and concentrates. The animals can be either 'grass finished' or 'yard finished' depending on the time of the year. Also the weight gain can be quite varied and target weight achieved between 14 to 20 months. (450 kgs. to 470 kgs).

*24 month grass fed beef*
As the system suggests, the animals are fed on grass (or silage) with no concentrates used. Target weights 500/550 kgs.

## Single Suckler Herd

Basically a one cow/one calf system with the mother rearing the calf for up to ten months. The calf is then sold out or 'fattened on' by the farmer. The advantage is the easy care of the calf with this natural system which makes husbandry easy. The disadvantage is financial – the cost of food for cow and calf to produce only one saleable animal per annum.

## Multiple Suckling

One cow looking after 2/3 calves or more. The major problem is the rejection of calves. Their welfare may lead to the enterprise becoming labour intensive.

## 3. SHEEP PRODUCTION

### Breeding.

The industry relies basically on a system of stratified cross-breeding from hill/upland sheep to produce a cross-ewe suitable for *lowland fat-lamb production:*

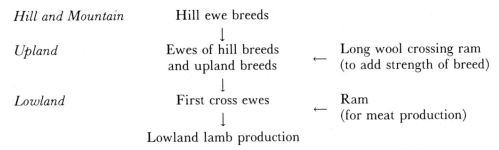

*Hill and Mountain*       Hill ewe breeds
$\downarrow$

*Upland*       Ewes of hill breeds   $\leftarrow$   Long wool crossing ram
       and upland breeds       (to add strength of breed)
$\downarrow$

*Lowland*       First cross ewes   $\leftarrow$   Ram
       $\downarrow$       (for meat production)
Lowland lamb production

Hence lowland sheep production concentrates on producing fat lambs for sale.

## Lowland Production

The farmer, in considering the annual production of the ewe, has a choice. He may aim for high prolificacy in a once per year breeding system or may try to reduce the lambing interval using less prolific ewes (i.e. fewer lambs at more frequent intervals). Most farmers go for the once per year spring lambing flock.

The Meat and Livestock Commission (MLC) keeps records of lambing percentages for different sheep breeds. The aim should be to produce a 200% lamb crop (an *average* of two lambs per ewe) but in practice the average is nearer 140%.

The age and condition of the ewe are very important factors. The number of lambs born increases with ewe maturity until six crops, after which the number will decrease. Also the ewe must be in good condition at 'tupping' (mating) but not over-fat. There is a deliberate policy to increase nutrition by 5% six weeks before 'tupping' to achieve a target weight of approximately 50 kgs. The ram is usually introduced in October; gestation is 20 weeks and lambs are born in March/April.

Another essential factor is to regulate the ewe's weight during pregnancy. The aim is not too much weight added until the last six weeks when the animal is fed with concentrates ('steaming-up'). Then good shepherding will be needed to avoid mortalities at birth and shortly after birth.

The main hazard in sheep production is disease and the rapid build up of parasites. Regular use of veterinary services is necessary and rotation of grazing fields advisable.

Profits depend on lambing percentage and weight gain from the lamb birth weight of 4/5 kgs. to a fat lamb dressed carcase weight of 18/20 kgs. Ewe replacements are usually at 10% to 20% of the ewe flock per annum. Rams are allocated at the rate of 1 to 50/60 ewes. Grassland management is again important and the stocking rate is usually between four and five ewes per acre (ten per hectare).

## 4. PIG PRODUCTION

There are two main areas to consider: *pig breeding* and *pig fattening*. Some farms will have pig breeding units, some farms pig fattening and some a complete system of breeding 'weaners' from the sow production herd, then fattening the weaners to pork; cutter; bacon, or heavy hog (farming terms used to indicate age and relative weight – see glossary on page 113).

## Pig Breeding

The main objective is to maximise the number of pigs reared per sow per annum. Therefore it is very important to keep to a minimum the days from the weaning of piglets to effective service of the sow. Gilts (females 6–12 months old) coming into the production herd are usually ready for mating at about 100kg. liveweight and 200 days of age.

Managing the mating of pigs is very important and the stockman's skills will have a dramatic effect on results achieved – the sows must be well tended and carefully housed. Nearby housing of an active boar will help to stimulate the onset of oestrus (the mating urge). Young boars will usually be ready soon after six months of age.

Feed of the sow and boar will tend to vary with genetic make-up but this will usually be not less than 1·8 kg. feed per day. *Feed costs* will represent a *major section of total costs* and this is therefore an important area for management control and recording. Piglet mortality is a hazard which every farmer tries to guard against but a mortality rate of 12% is not unusual. The aim should be to reduce this as far as possible. The breeding sow herd will call for replacements at about 30% per annum as the usual average is six litters per sow per lifetime.

### Production standards

|  | *Average* | *High* | *Target* |
|---|---|---|---|
| Weaners sold per sow per annum. |  |  |  |
| 3 week weaning | 19 | 22 | 24 |
| 5 week weaning | 17·5 | 20 | 22 |
| 8 week weaning | 15 | 18 | 20 |
|  |  |  |  |
| Pigs born alive per litter | 10 | 10·5 | 11 |
| Pigs weaned per litter | 8·5 | 9·5 | 10 |
| Feed per sow per annum | 1·5t. to | 1·25t. |  |

## Pig Fattening

(For selling-out weights see graph on page 20)

Again the stockman has a very important part to play. Mortality risks are still high through disease possibilities – particularly with the intensive housing systems now operated. Feed costs are again the main part of input costs and the *food conversion ratio* is usually monitored, i.e. the amount of food to produce 1kg. of pig. Obviously the lower the figure the better the FCR will be.

### FCR
*(kgs. per kg. of weight gain)*

|  | *Average* | *Good* | *Target* |
|---|---|---|---|
| Pork | 2·9 | 2·6 | 2·4 |
| Cutter | 3·1 | 2·8 | 2·6 |
| Bacon | 3·2 | 3·0 | 2·9 |
| Heavy Hog | 3·9 | 3·5 | 3·4 |

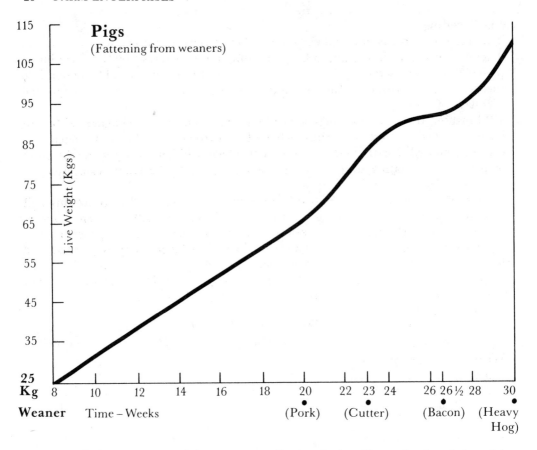

## Pigs
(Fattening from weaners)

Live Weight (Kgs)

Time – Weeks

Weaner

(Pork)    (Cutter)    (Bacon)    (Heavy Hog)

Feeding of a 'barley-mix' (a very cost-effective feedstuff) to pigs has led to the dominant areas of pig production being located in the Eastern Counties (the arable production areas).

After farrowing the piglets stay with the sow for three to eight weeks, but more producers are now looking at early weaning (three weeks) to give maximum production levels.

### Feed use (Fattening from Weaners)
*(In Kgs.)*

|          | Average | Good | Target |
|----------|---------|------|--------|
| Pork     | 150     | 135  | 130    |
| Cutter   | 235     | 210  | 195    |
| Bacon    | 255     | 230  | 215    |
| Heavy hog| 380     | 350  | 240    |

### In Summary

Remember the key areas in pig production: stockmanship; management control; food conversion ratio and feed costs.

# 5. CEREALS

## Wheat, Barley and Oats

This is an important sector of farming with a total land useage of 3·9m. hectares (9·6m. acres). The best way to gain knowledge of it is to visit farms at different times during the winter to spring months and observe the different growth stages of the plants.

The main factors affecting cereal profitability are yield, input costs, location and time of sowing. The rainfall area, soil type and geographical aspect of the farm will give some farmers a head-start over others. Yields of 10t. per hectare (4t. per acre) may well be the norm in East Anglia but one would certainly not expect the same in the Sussex Wealden clay areas!

The time of sowing is very important. Generally speaking, the earlier the sowing, the higher the yield. Winter-sown crops will outyield spring-sown but input costs will be higher.

As a guideline:

*Winter Barley and Oats* – sow mid September to October
*Winter Wheat*          – sow late September (light soils) to mid October
*Spring Cereals*        – sow late February to mid March

Sowing needs to be in a good seedbed whether done by 'direct drilling' or more traditional methods e.g. ploughing and 'broadcasting'. There must be an adequate supply of phosphate and potash with nitrogen levels adjusted to the fertility conditions. Uniformity in depth of sowing and distribution of seed are obviously important to *maximise the potential yield* from the land by achieving a sufficient level of plant population. Chemical control of weeds, diseases and pests has improved in recent years. This development together with better varieties of seed has led to improved yields.

*Herbicides* will control annual and perennial broad leaved weeds, and grass weeds – couch, watergrass, wild oats, blackgrass, meadow grasses and sterile brome.

*Fungicides* will control diseases such as mildew, rusts, leaf blotch, eye-spot and septoria.

*Pesticides* will control aphids, slugs, leather jackets, eelworms etc.

Bankers cannot expect to be experts on crop diseases but the photographs on the centre pages should help you identify some of the major cereal crop diseases.

Wheel damage to growing crops has led to some farmers 'tramlining'. This is a planned system of wheel-ways through the crop to accommodate spraying etc. This also helps to speed up operations as the planned 'route' will be following each time. However, some land is just not suitable for tramlining as it may result in heavy rutting. Protection to the crops is therefore very important, whether it is from disease, from weeds or from machine damage. All must be controlled in an effort to maximise yields.

A final point to note is that, although cereal harvesting may be in August, before the sale proceeds of the crop are received, the farmer may well be needing to finance the input costs of his next year's crop!

## 6. GRASSLAND PRODUCTION

Grass is an important area of farm management. It is a crop which can be grown relatively easily in our climate and the main attraction is the low cost of grazed grass as feed compared with other animal feeds. The objective is to produce fresh grass, hay, silage, or (machine prepared) dried grass. This can be achieved by planting 'leys' (temporary grass) or permanent pasture. The performance of permanent pasture is highly variable from very poor rough grazing to excellent grazing depending on soil fertility and topography. If grass leys are sown then a common combination is perennial ryegrass and Italian ryegrass. The mixture will depend very much on the length of ley to be established – the Italian ryegrass is generally more suited to short-term leys and can give early heavy yields for silage at the first cut (end of May/early June).

'D' value is a measurement of the level of digestibility of the organic matter in the dry matter of the plant. It is measured by chemical analysis. The amount which an animal grazes per day will determine the energy intake for body maintenance and production (e.g. in the case of a dairy cow). The best results will be obtained from dairy cows and beef cattle when 'D' values of grazing are about 65–70.

### Silage

The preparation of silage is a method of storing herbage for winter feeding. First cuts of grass are usually in May or early June with the objective of not less than 65D anticipated 'D' value. This first cut can yield 8/9 tons of made silage per acre whereas second cuts in July/August will yield less – perhaps 4/5 tons. Silage is usually made by storing the chopped grass in a pit or in a 'clamp' under polythene sheeting.

Silage-making under polythene sheeting depends on the action of the soluble carbohydrates of the herbage being fermented by the addition of lactic acid. This 'pickles' the grass. Sugar levels affect fermentation – if they are too low then additives will be needed. Silage analysis is recommended to check on the quality of feed produced.

### Hay

This is still the most common of winter feeds, but hay making is more dependent on good weather than silage-making as it is usually made by natural field drying. Most hay is therefore made in June which should be the driest month! The aim is to dry as quickly as possible then store at about 18% moisture content.

### Dried Grass

This is the least popular feedstuff due to the high capital outlay needed for processing by way of special machinery. If the farmer does not process his own, then packing and transport costs will be an additional expense.

**Systems of Grazing**

These are three basic systems, the choice of which will depend on the lay-out of the farm.

    i  *Rotational grazing* is widely used, particularly for dairy cows. The idea is to use either paddocks of varying sizes or alternatively 'strip-grazing' which is in effect a moveable paddock where the area grazed by the animals is controlled by an electric fence. This system obviously requires more day-to-day decisions and labour.

    ii  *Set-stocking* involves animals freely grazing in a series of fields, or in a field without restriction. This is a simple system to operate and widely used for beef grazing and sheep. Planning the stocking rate of animals to the grazing area is very important to avoid possible low output with this system.

    iii  *Zero-Grazing* depends on cutting the herbage and carting it to stock that are housed in yards. This system will naturally involve high operating costs.

## IN CONCLUSION

In this Chapter I have given a few details on:

    Dairy production
    Beef production
    Sheep production
    Pigs – breeding and fattening
    Cereals
    Grassland

I hope these will help you in your approach to the farmer. The best way to learn is to go and see the farm!

CHAPTER 3

# Farm Financial Planning

Farm financial planning has become even more important over recent years owing to the squeeze on profit margins. Farm input costs have been rising faster than the unit values received for the commodity sold. This has led to a greater awareness by the farmer of the necessity for improved farm planning to maximise the use of his resources in both land and finance.

The most widely used technique by both farm business advisors and the more progressive farmers is the gross margin system.

## GROSS MARGIN SYSTEM

A farm business will normally consist of several different enterprises. Each enterprise will have costs specifically related to that enterprise and also other costs which are shared over the total farm business. Allocation of a portion of all farming costs to a specific enterprise can be completely misleading when making planning decisions. For example, when an enterprise is expanded or contracted, or terminated, the variable costs for such an enterprise will vary roughly in proportion to the size of that enterprise, i.e. the variable costs tend to be volume orientated. Many fixed costs will stay the same.

Hence we have identified in farming two categories of costs:

    i Variable costs
    ii Fixed costs

Variable costs are easy to allocate as they will change with the scale of enterprise (volume orientated). Fixed costs are not easy to allocate and do not necessarily change directly with the scale of the enterprise. Examples of variable costs are:

*Winter Wheat* – seed, fertilisers, sprays.
*Dairy Cows*    – concentrate foods, forage costs, veterinary fees and medicine, artificial insemination, straw etc.

Examples of fixed costs: rent, regular labour, machinery and motive power, miscellaneous farm costs.

## Calculating the Gross Margin

The gross margin itself is the total in gross output of an enterprise less the variable costs. GROSS OUTPUT LESS VARIABLE COSTS = GROSS MARGIN as in the following examples:

### Example A (Winter Wheat)

|  |  | £/acre |
|---|---|---|
| Output 42 cwt per acre at £112 per ton |  | 235 |
| *Less variable costs* |  |  |
| Seed | 14 |  |
| Fertilizer | 26 |  |
| Sprays | 25 |  |
| Total variable costs per acre |  | 65 |
| Gross margin per acre |  | 170 |

### Example B (Dairy Cows)

|  |  | £ |
|---|---|---|
| Milk sales per cow, |  |  |
| 1,100 gallons at 58p per gallon |  | 638 |
| *Less* cost of replacing cows |  | (38) |
| Plus calf sale |  | 75 |
| Output |  | 675 |
| *Variable costs £/cow* |  |  |
| Concentrates | 238 |  |
| Forage costs | 45 |  |
| Bedding | 7 |  |
| Vetinary and Medicine | 12 |  |
| A.I. & enterprise recording fees | 10 |  |
| Consumable dairy stores etc. | 13 |  |
| Total variable costs |  | 325 |
| Gross Margin |  | £350  per cow |

Having looked at gross margins for two enterprises we now follow the same procedure for all the enterprises on the farm in question and then deduct fixed costs to give a trading margin (see Figure I opposite).

**FIGURE I**

GROSS MARGIN BUDGET

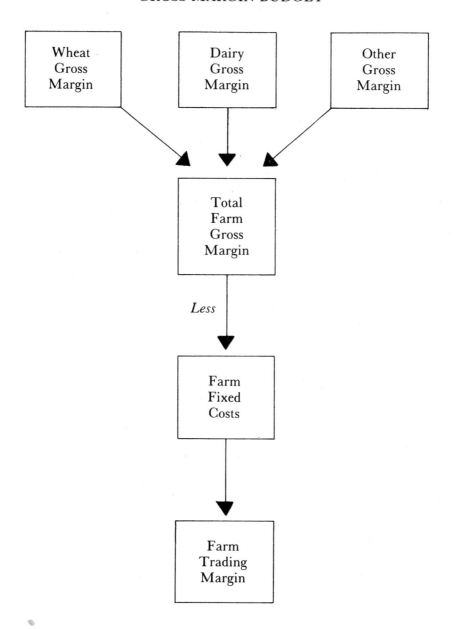

**FIGURE II**

FARM FINANCIAL PLANNING

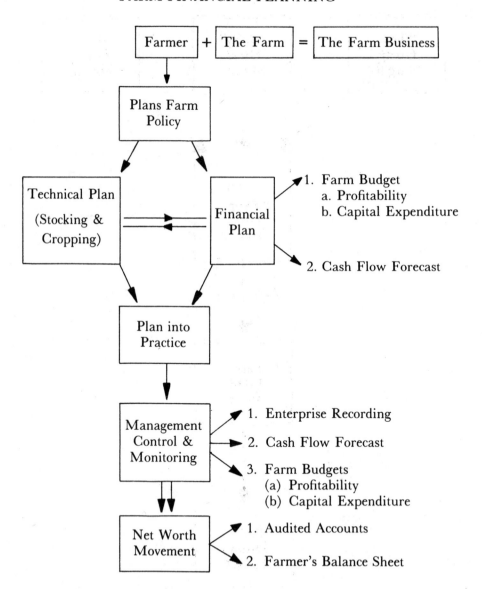

Referring to Figure II (on page 28) we can see that the farmer, having due regard for the structure and soil type of his farm, can draw up a *technical plan* for the stocking and cropping of the farm. Having formulated his plan he will then, using the Gross Margin techniques described earlier, calculate a farm budget for profitability (see Fig. III on page 30).

This budget must of course be based on *realistic* levels of expected technical performance. It must not be over optimistic and should reflect past achievements on the farm. Then, as a footnote to the budget or alternatively as a separate budget, items of capital expenditure should be listed. These farm budgets then form the basis for the cash flow forecast which is similar to any other business CFF in that it lists receipts and payments over 12 months and the timing of those entries will affect the bank account balance.

Let us be quite clear:

THE FARM BUDGET INDICATES PLANNED PROFITABILITY based on the stocking and cropping plan.

THE CASH FLOW FORECAST INDICATES THE FEASIBILITY of the plan, in cash terms.

Provided all looks well the farmer can then put his plans into practice. If he runs into a negative position in his cash flow forecast then, unless this can be restructured, he will of course need the help of his bank or other sources of credit. (We shall look at cash flow forecasts in more detail in Chapter 4.)

## Management Control and Monitoring

The farmer having formulated plans and put them into practice should monitor the farm progress. It is not sufficient to organise the farm work daily. Performance levels should be checked regularly against budget, receipts and payments recorded on the cash flow forecast and compared with targets. Early indication of possible problems can then be seen and action taken.

**FIGURE III**

## FARM BUDGET FOR PROFITABILITY
### (Example of Layout)

| Enterprise | No. of Stock/Area Cropped | Gross Margin | Total £ |
|---|---|---|---|
| | | | |

Farm Gross Margin _____

*Less fixed costs*
   Labour
   Power & machinery
   Rent & rates
   Sundries

TRADING MARGIN    £ _____

*To meet commitments:*
   Personal drawings
   Bank finance charges
   H.P./Leasing
   Taxation
   Capital Investment

Extending this gross margin budget (Fig. III) numerically on a hypothetical 600 acre cereal/dairy farm rented at £26 per acre could give:

| **Gross Margin Budget** | *per annum* |
|---|---:|
| | £ |
| Wheat: 230 acres @ £173 (G.M. per acre) | 39,790 |
| Dairy cows: 120 @ £350 (G.M. per cow) | 42,000 |
| Dairy herd replacements: 30 @ £200 (G.M. per heifer) | 6,000 |
| Spring barley: 120 acres @ £120 (G.M. per acre) | 14,400 |
| TOTAL FARM GROSS MARGIN | £102,190 |

*Less fixed costs*

| | |
|---|---:|
| rent, labour, machinery etc. | 78,600 |
| TRADING MARGIN | £23,590 |

## NET WORTH MOVEMENT

Surely the success or failure of all the farmer's plans must at the end of each year be indicated in the resulting net worth (or capital) position. Many farmers seem to forget this!

The net worth can be monitored effectively in two simple ways:

*Audited Accounts*
Although probably out of date, these do indicate profits being earned and retentions in the farm business.

*Farmer's Balance Sheet** (or statement of assets and liabilities)
Again net worth can be monitored by simply totalling assets less liabilities at a similar date annually. Most banks have a form for this and a typical example is illustrated in Fig. IV (see pages 33–35).

In completing the form, the farmer should use estimated market values to give a true net worth position. Comparison with the previous year's statement will then indicate the net worth movement in the farm business. An increase in net worth should reflect profits earned and retained in the business, after allowing for any increased valuation in freehold land.

**Summary**

In farm planning:

Complete:
    i the technical plan (stocking & cropping)
    ii the financial plans:
        farm budgets
        cash flow forecast
        farmer's balance sheet

*Sometimes also called Stock and Crop Form or Farmer's Confidential Statement.

Then:
iii Monitor and control
iv Check resulting net worth.

Practical examples using these financial planning techniques are given in the following chapter.

**FIGURE IV**

FARMER'S BALANCE SHEET
(example of lay-out)

Name:                              Bank:

Farm
  Address:

| Farm area | OWNED | TENANTED |
|---|---|---|
| CROPS | | |
| GRASS | | |
| WOODLAND & ROUGHLAND | | |
| TOTAL | | |

Rent
Payable £

Landlord:

ESTIMATED EFFECTIVE ACREAGE:

**Livestock**

Cattle (Nos.)                    (Market Value)              *Total Value*

                @
                @
                @
Pigs
                @
                @
                @
Sheep
                @
                @
                @
Others

                                              TOTAL     £ ____

**PRODUCE FOR OWN CONSUMPTION**
(Silage, Corn, Hay, Etc)
                @ per ton
                @ per ton

                                              TOTAL     £ ____

**FIGURE IV** (cont'd)

**Growing Crops**
(value usually at cost of variable inputs only

| Acres | Crop | | Total value |
|---|---|---|---|
| | | @ | |
| | | @ | |
| | | @ | |
| | | @ | |
| | | @ | |
| | | TOTAL   £ | |

---

**Stored Produce for Sale**

| Crop | Tons | (Market value) | Total value |
|---|---|---|---|
| | | @ | |
| | | @ | |
| | | @ | |
| | | @ | |
| | | TOTAL   £ | |

---

**Farm Machinery**

| Date of purchase | Item | Cost | Market Value |
|---|---|---|---|
| | | | |
| | | TOTAL   £ | |

**FIGURE IV** (cont'd)

| Liabilities | £ | Assets | £ |
|---|---|---|---|
| Rent outstanding<br>Due to Bank<br>  – Current account<br>  – Loan account<br>Creditors<br>Hire Purchase<br>Private loans (short-term) | | Cash at bank<br>Debtors<br>Grant due<br>Stock<br>  – Produce for sale<br>  – Livestock<br>  – Produce for own<br>    consumption<br>  – Fertiliser/seed/feed, etc.<br>Valuation<br>  – Growing Crops<br>  – Tenant right* | |
| SUB TOTAL | | SUB TOTAL | |
| Mortgages<br>Dilapidations<br>Other liabilities | | Land and buildings<br>  acres @ £<br>Farm Machinery<br>Tenant's improvements* | |
| LIABILITIES | | | |
| Date | | | |
| **Net worth/balance** | | | |
| £ | | TOTAL   £ | |

**Other Items:**

1. Contingent liabilities:
2. Leasing:
3. Non-farming assets:

*'Tenant right' is, in short, the value of improvements made to the farmland, usually valued by a professional land agent. 'Tenant's improvements', i.e. to fixed assets such as buildings, will affect the value of the tenancy and should only be made with the landlord's permission.

CHAPTER 4

# Assessing the Agricultural Lending Proposition

## BASIC POINTS TO CONSIDER

In looking at a lending proposition in farming you must surely take the same general starting points as with any business proposition. The first aspects to consider will be the MAN and his BUSINESS. Then the amount of money requested – is it adequate? Can it be repaid? What if things go wrong? As with other lending, there is no mathematical formula to make life very easy (and probably boring)! Every farm is different – in structure, size, layout and facilities.

The financial resources of the business will also vary as between farms. It is a different proposition to lend £20,000 to a farm business with total assets of say £100,000 than to lend the same amount to one with total assets of £20,000. Also if you lend £20,000 to buy more dairy cows, then the cash return to the business will be different from £20,000 lent to buy a new tractor which may only 'return' less costs in fuel, repairs etc.

The five basic points to consider for any type of bank lending (agriculture or otherwise) are:

1. How much is required?
2. What is to be done with the money?
3. What are the plans for repayment?
4. What will be the bank's position if the plans for repayment go wrong?
5. What is the experience and track record of the borrower?

If you look again at Fig. II – *Farm Financial Planning* in Chapter 3 – then it should be possible to answer the five questions from the documents essential in farm financial planning. If these are all not available then get your farmer, or his agricultural adviser, to complete them!

   i  *The Cash Flow Forecast* will tell us what is to be done with the money and how much is required.

  ii  The plans for repayment will be illustrated in the *Cash Flow Forecast* and the feasibility of any repayments shown by looking at any margin available in the *Farm Budget* together with the record of past profits in the *Audited Accounts*.

iii  If things go wrong, then the 'buffer' or net worth is illustrated in the past *Audited Accounts* and the up-to-date net worth position in the *Farmer's Balance Sheet*.

## VISITING THE FARM

This is as essential as with any other business. You will glean a lot of information. Most farmers I have found to be very receptive and only too willing to show you around their farm. It is usually their pride and joy!

Observation and discussion will enable you to make a judgement as to the technical and management ability of the farmer. What is his experience? How long has he been at the farm? Does he use modern techniques? Is he in full control or does he spend a lot of time away from the farm? What is his depth of management ability and who is there to help him? Does he delegate routine tasks? Who keeps the farm records?

Also you will see the farm size and learn about the stocking and cropping of the farm, the land and soil types, the layout of the farm, the state of buildings and machinery. Does the place look well kept and well organised? Are the hedges trimmed, fences in good repair, ditches clear? Do the animals look healthy and well fed? Are the crops looking good or are they full of weeds and disease? Have the buildings and machinery the capacity to meet the farmer's plans? Look at the farmer's stocking and cropping plans and discuss them.

All this information will help you when going on to contemplate the *financial picture* of the farm business. A checklist *(aide memoire)* for recording a farm visit is given in Appendix 4.

## FINANCIAL PERFORMANCE

This is where the banker is fortunate. He has all the usual bank records available to him. Examination of the bank statements will reveal the business turnover, the average bank balance, the range of the account, standing orders and direct debits and any unpaid cheques.

Comparison of these statistics with previous years will help paint the financial picture e.g. falling turnover coupled with an increasing debit balance will merit close investigation!

## LOOKING AT ASSET COVER

### 1. Audited Accounts

The accounts may well be historic but it is well worth looking at the Balance Sheet.

The following simplified balance sheet illustrates what can be revealed and whether certain items might require further investigation.

| Liabilities | £ | Assets | |
|---|---|---|---|
| Rent outstanding | 3,500 | Debtors | 2,000 |
| Bank | 14,400 | Stock | 40,320 |
| Creditors | 3,150 | Tenant right | 5,000 |
| | 21,050 (b) | | 47,320 (d) |
| Capital/Net worth | 30,070 (c) | Farm machinery | 3,800 |
| | 51,120 | | 51,120 (a) |

    i *Total assets* (a) – are there any intangibles or fictitious assets?

    ii *Total debts* (b) – debt structure – long/short-term?

    iii *Total assets* (a): *total debts* (b) – debts should be well covered.

    iv *Net Worth* (c) – i.e. total assets minus total debts. This is the margin or buffer for the business. (This could well be understated.)

    v *Total assets* (a): *current assets* (d) – what is the proportion of quickly realisable assets?

    vi *Current assets* (d): *total debts* (b) – this represents the liquidity of the business. Can current debts be repaid without resorting to sale of fixed assets?

Then, after examining the trading and profit and loss account record:

    i *Stock: sales turnover* – dependent on type of farm enterprises.

    ii *Debtors: sales* – debtors figure in farming should be well covered.

    iii *Profits* – are they being earned and retained? Look at the resulting profit and loss account balance.

Then, the bank lending:

    i *Net worth: bank lending* – (This will be discussed in more detail later under Farmer's Balance Sheets).

    ii *Net Worth: total liabilities* – Is the balance being maintained or deteriorating?

All of these ratios become more meaningful when you *compare trends over several years'* balance sheets. It is dangerous to make a judgment on the year's figures in isolation.

## 2. Limitations of Audited Accounts

Some of the limitations are:

(a) The accounts are often prepared for taxation purposes only. They may therefore not give a true indication of the net worth of the business. Land, buildings and machinery may well be undervalued on a cost *less* depreciation basis.

*Stock* may be undervalued and the accountant could accept the farmer's valuation without verifying this.

*Sales* invoices could be carried forward into the next accounting period – therefore reducing profits earned.

(b) There may be long delays between the date of audit and the date to which the accounts refer. They may well be 12/18 months out of date before the bank sees them!

(c) Individual firms of accountants may apply different interpretations to certain items in the accounts.

(d) The basis of valuation of a number of items may differ from the current value, as explained later in Chapter 7 on Taxation.

An example of a farmer's audited accounts is given in Appendix 5.

This brings us to the Farmer's Balance Sheet.

## 3. The Farmer's Balance Sheet

As explained in the previous chapter, this management document is simply an *up-to-date* statement of assets and liabilities. It is designed to give an up-to-date assessment of the NET WORTH of the farm business based on realistic market valuations. It is important to take a consistent attitude to valuations. These can be checked against the *Farmers Weekly* or other agricultural journals.

## *EXAMPLE – FARMER A*

Take the Farmer's Balance Sheet of Farmer A dated August 1981 (see pages 41–43). This provides considerably more management information about the farm business than the audited accounts.

**FARMER A**

## FARMER'S BALANCE SHEET

NAME: Farmer A                    DATE: August 1981

BANK: A Bank

FARM ADDRESS: WEST SUSSEX

FARM AREA

| | Owned | Tenanted |
|---|---|---|
| Crops | | 62 |
| Grass | | 270 |
| Woodland and Roughland | | 13 |
| Total | | 345 |

Rent Payable: £6,400

Landlord: Mr. Jones

ESTIMATED EFFECTIVE ACREAGE: 320

**Livestock**

| Cattle (Nos.) | | (Market Value) £ | Total Value £ |
|---|---|---|---|
| 100 Dairy cows | @ | 425 | 42,500 |
| 20 Heifers | @ | 400 | 8,000 |
| 60 Young Stock | @ | 250 | 15,000 |
| Pigs | | | |
| 20 Sows | @ | 80 | 1,600 |
| 40 Weaners | @ | 20 | 800 |
| Sheep | | | |
| 200 Ewes | @ | 40 | 8,000 |
| 180 Lambs | @ | 25 | 4,500 |
| Others | | | |
| | | Total | £80,400 |

## PRODUCE FOR OWN CONSUMPTION

| (Silage, Corn, Hay etc.) | | Total Value £ |
|---|---|---|
| 30t. Hay | @ £40 per ton | 1,200 |
| 200t. Silage | @ £10 per ton | 2,000 |
| | Total | £3,200 |

**FARMER A (Cont'd)**

**Growing Crops**

(Value usually at cost of variable inputs only)

| Acres | Crop | £ | Total Value £ |
|---|---|---|---|
| 20 | Winter Wheat | @ 65 | 1,300 |
| 12 | Spring Barley | @ 48 | 576 |
|  |  | @ |  |
|  |  | @ |  |
|  |  | @ |  |
|  |  |  | £1,876 |

**Stored Produce for sale**

| Crop | Tons |  | (Market Value) £ | Total Value £ |
|---|---|---|---|---|
| Barley | 45t. | @ | 90 | 4,050 |
|  |  | @ |  |  |
|  |  | @ |  |  |
|  |  | @ |  |  |
|  |  |  |  | £4,050 |

**Farm Machinery**

| Date of Purchase | Item | Cost £ | Market Value £ |
|---|---|---|---|
| 1978 | 2 Tractors | 3,400 | 8,000 |
| Various other items |  |  | 5,000 |
|  | TOTAL |  | £13,000 |

**FARMER A** (Cont'd)

| Liabilities | £ | Assets | £ |
|---|---|---|---|
| Rent outstanding | 2,000 | Cash at bank | — |
| Due to Bank | | Debtors | 2,000 |
| – Current Account | 8,900 | Grants due | — |
| – Loan Account | 5,000 | Stock | |
| Creditors | 2,150 | – Produce for sale | 4,050 |
| Hire Purchase | Nil | – Livestock | 80,400 |
| Private Loans | Nil | – Produce for own | |
| (short term) | | consumption | 3,200 |
| | | – Fertiliser/seed/feed | |
| | | etc. | 3,850 |
| | | Valuation | |
| | | – Growing Crops | 1,876 |
| | | – Tenant right | 5,000 |
| Sub-total | 18,050 | Sub-total | 100,376 |
| Mortgages | — | Land & Buildings | |
| Dilapidations | — | acres @ £ | — |
| Other Liabilities | — | Farm Machinery | 13,000 |
| Liabilities | 18,050 | Tenants improvements | — |
| Date | | | |
| August 1981 | | | |
| **Net Worth/Balance** | 95,326 | | |
| | £113,376 | Total | £113,376 |

**Other Items:**

1. Contingent liabilities:  Nil
2. Leasing:  Nil
3. Non-farming assets:  Life policies, surrender values £8,000
4. Savings account:  £5,000

The tenure of land is indicated (Farmer A is a tenant). The acreage is stated together with rent payable and the split between crops and grass. Then, the livestock are valued and it can be seen that this is mainly a dairy farm with sheep and pigs and a small corn acreage. Totalling livestock units at appropriate stocking rates and adding on the crops, the farm acreage being farmed can be roughly checked, depending on the time of the year..

The final summary shows a *net worth of £95,326*. This looks a healthy balance relative to the total debts at £18,050 and bank borrowing at £13,900. Looking at the assets the main item is the livestock at £80,400. There is little else other than farm machinery. From an asset cover viewpoint the bank borrowing is well covered but this does not indicate business *profitability*. We will look at this a little later.

Compare the Farmer's Balance Sheet figures with the latest audited accounts (see below). What is the net worth difference? Why? Any other significant differences? Check creditors – this figure could be understated by the farmer!

## FARMER A

### BALANCE SHEET
(Audited on historic cost accounting basis)

| Liabilities | £ | Assets | £ |
|---|---|---|---|
| Rent outstanding | 3,500 | Debtors | 2,000 |
| Bank | 14,400 | Stock | 40,320 |
| Creditors | 3,150 | Tenant right | 5,000 |
|  | ——— | Farm machinery | 3,800 |
|  | 21,050 |  |  |
|  |  |  |  |
| Capital/Net worth | 30,070 |  |  |
|  | ——— |  | ——— |
|  | 51,120 | Total Assets | 51,120 |

The significant differences compared with the Farmer's Balance Sheet on page 43 are:

*Total assets:*   £51,120 compared with £113,376
*Net worth:*   £30,070 compared with  £95,326
*Stock:*   £40,320 compared with  £91,500

> This results from using market values in the Farmer's Balance Sheet – the audited accounts will show the *lower* of cost or market value.

*Farm Machinery:* £3,800 compared with £13,000

> (The result, again, of using market values as opposed to the usual formula of cost *less* depreciation.)

(a) *Net worth* trends can be compared by looking at a series of farmer's balance sheets. No change can take place without some reason. Thus net worth is very important to monitor and changes should be investigated. A steady rise in net worth is most encouraging but still needs investigation.

Is a rising trend in net worth due to profit being earned and retained? It may be due to a revaluation of assets or a refund of taxation. Alternatively there may have been a sale of machinery not previously included in the farm valuation in the balance sheet!

### (b) *Asset Structure*

Land values far outweigh earning capacity. Taking our previous example and making Farmer A the *owner* of 345 acres rather than the tenant, the difference in the value of total assets is staggering! Value 345 acres at say £1,500 per acre = £517,500. The total assets are then £628,876.

For this reason freehold property in farming must be considered separately from the other assets being used. Hence we look at farmer's balance sheets on a tenant's asset basis for comparative purposes. In our example Farmer A has total assets of £113,376. Dividing this by the effective farm acreage of 320 acres gives us a figure of £354 tenants assets per acre.

This can be compared with standard data; or, better still, you can *build up your own file of tenants assets/acre in your area*. This is most useful when handling an approach by a farmer going in for a new farm or expanding his farm by taking on extra land. The following is a data survey of the South East:

| Farm Type Group | Range of Total Tenants Capital | |
| --- | --- | --- |
| | *Per Hectare* | *(Per Acre)* |
| Mainly dairying | £1,115–1,555 | (£450–£630) |
| Mainly arable | £835–£1,045 | (£340–£425) |
| Dairy & arable | £955–£955 | (£385–£405) |
| Mainly sheep/cattle | £715–£1,150 | (£290–£465) |
| Sheep/cattle & arable | £725–£890 | (£295–£360) |

(Source: *Farm Management Pocket Book* by John Nix, Wye College (University of London), 1982.)

You can see, therefore, that the *average* value of tenant's assets per acre in this survey is £400. An owner occupier will of course require tenants-type assets to stock and run the farm in addition to the land asset owned.

Therefore, if you are looking at an owner-occupier balance sheet, you would expect to see total assets in the region of £1,900–£2,000 per acre dependent of course on the land valuation and the type of farm (i.e. tenant's assets £400 per acre *plus* land value £1,500/£1,600 per acre).

*Return on Capital employed* is covered in Chapter 5.

### (c) *Gearing*

This is the relationship between *total borrowings and net worth*. The business is said to be 'highly geared' when the proportion of borrowed money is high relative to the net worth of the business and 'low geared' when in the opposite situation. For total borrowings, I would include all borrowed funds irrespective of length of credit allowed.

For tenant farmers my experience has been that when the total borrowings approach the net worth, i.e. 1:1 gearing, then the farmer must be very good in technical and management capability to cope with this high level of gearing. *There is however no 'proper' ratio* – so much can depend on the individual farm business and effectiveness of management.

When you add the complication of freehold property values then, as stated earlier, the net worth will become far greater and the gearing will become meaningless. *It is then that the banker must look again to the level of profits earned and to be earned, toether with the cash flow generated, to determine the prudent gearing level.*

## LOOKING AT 'SERVICEABILITY'

In assessing the farmer's capacity to meet his commitments and service his borrowing, as well as looking at the past profit records and trends in net worth, examination of farm enterprise recordings is useful to see more up-to-date progress. In our example, Farmer A could be recording his dairy herd on a Milk Marketing Board Scheme or I.C.I. Dairymaid Scheme. Figures will be available usually up to the end of the previous month in a very detailed analysis of input costs and output (per cow) for all the herds – identified only by code number – in his area. Examination will indicate not only month by month costs and output, but also 'rolling' averages', i.e. annual averages updated month by month.

He will thus be able to monitor his herd performance and compare it with that of other local farmers.

### 1. Quick Guidelines for Serviceability

There are methods which will quickly identify the financial pressures that the farm business will face:

(a) *Rent and Finance Charges* (Rental equivalent)
This is useful as a guideline for tenants and owner-occupiers or a combination of both. It takes into account *all financial commitments* plus the rent payable and thereby removes the distinction between the tenant and owner. It is very useful to discuss this with the farmer who usually has a 'gut feeling' as to the level of rental equivalent per acre that he can cope with successfully. The figure is calculated by including the following charges *per annum:*

    i Rent and rates.
    ii Bank overdraft interest.
    iii Bank loans – interest and capital repayments.
    iv Agricultural Mortgage Corporation – interest and capital repayments.
    v Hire-purchase charges.
    vi Leasing charges.
    vii Merchant credit charges.
    viii Private loans – interest and capital.

This total is then divided by the effective acreage.

*EXAMPLE*

| Using Farmer A figures: | | £ |
|---|---|---|
| Rent | | 6,400 |
| Bank overdraft average balance – | | |
| say £4,000 debit @ 15% | | 600 |
| Loan capital & interest | | 1,400 |
| | Total | £8,400 |

Divided by 320 = *£26 per acre.*

The interpretation of this rental equivalent depends on the type of the farm and farming system. As a general guide *£50 per acre* is often talked of as a figure below which servicing should not be too difficult. Above £50 per acre needs a closer look. This is only a general guideline – so be careful!

It is best, in my opinion, as with tenants assets per acre, to *build up your own file on rental equivalents.* I have done this for my own county, and the variations which occur between different types of farm becomes more apparent. (Note: a specimen bank form for reviewing a farming customer's account is given in Appendix 6.)

**Survey of Rental Equivalents**

| Farm type | Average of Sizes | Break-even Rental equivalent per acre | |
|---|---|---|---|
| | | *Average* | *High* |
| Cereal farm | 450 acres | £53 | £79 |
| Dairy farm | 260 acres | £50 | £76 |
| Cereals/Dairy | 600 acres | £44 | £73 |
| Beef/Sheep | 300 acres | £37 | £51 |
| Arable | 700 acres | £57 | £97 |

These break-even figures suggest for example that an average cereal farmer on 450 acres could cope with a maximum rental equivalent of £53 per acre whereas a good farmer could cope with £79 per acre.

The beef/sheep farmer – average: £37 per acre
                                        – good: £51 per acre.

*Thus the rental equivalent figure is only a quick reference guideline* in assessing the likely financial pressure.

(b) *Rental equivalent as a percentage of gross output.*
The rental equivalent yardstick takes no account of the output of the business but this new measurement looks at rental equivalent as a percentage of farm gross output. The farm gross output is the net of total farm returns *plus* the value of produce consumed in the farmhouse or supplied to workers, *less* purchases of livestock and other products bought for resale.

Guidelines are:
    i less than 10% – there should be little problem.
    ii between 10% and 15% is the usual range.
    iii 15%–20% is getting tighter and needs a closer look.
    iv 20% or more is considered high

*Example*
Farmer A's rent and finance charges totalled £8,400. Let us assume his farm business gross output is £103,500 per annum. The rental equivalent as a percentage of gross output is therefore 8% (a low charge).

## 2. Farm Budgets

The guidelines we have looked at, i.e. rental equivalent and rental equivalent as a percentage of gross output are only quick measurements. The total serviceability picture can be seen far more clearly when examining the total farm budget. Some farmers argue that budgets are a waste of time. My answer is that any budget is better than none! They are certainly essential in planning the *profitability* of the farm.

If the farmer cannot prepare farm budgets himself there are many people prepared to assist. The first point of reference is the Ministry of Agriculture (Agricultural Development and Advisory Service) (ADAS) which has offices throughout the country. There is also the Milk Marketing Board, ICI, and the Meat and Livestock Commission, and certain firms of accountants – all have advisers trained to help the farmer. Some commercial suppliers of fertilizers, feedstuffs etc. also have specialist advisory services.

ADAS will also give the farmer detailed technical advice on land useage, enterprises, soil analysis, suitability of buildings, grants available, and classified results for comparison with individual farms. The ADAS adviser will also help with the completion of cash flow forecasts and capital expenditure budgets if required. *All the advisers use the same gross margin techniques for farm budgets* and although the layout may differ; provided you understand gross margins (See Chapter 3), you should be able to understand any farm budget presented to you.

For examples of different types of farm budget presentations see:
    Appendix 7 – Milk Marketing Board Forward Budget
    Appendix 8 – ADAS Gross Margin Analysis
    Appendix 9 – Meat and Livestock Commission – Beefplan Report.

*Example*
Returning to our old friend Farmer A, it may help to refresh your memory on farm enterprises. Here is a farm budget which could be presented:

## FARMER A

### GROSS MARGIN BUDGET ACCOUNT 1981/82

| Enterprise | | Gross Margin | | Total |
|---|---|---|---|---|
| | | £ | | £ |
| 100 Dairy cows | @ | 337 | | 33,700 |
| 20 Dairy replacements | @ | 271 | | 5,420 |
| 20 Sows | @ | 171 | | 3,420 |
| 200 Ewes | @ | 33 | | 6,600 |
| 20 Acres winter wheat | @ | 186 | | 3,720 |
| 12 Acres spring barley | @ | 136 | | 1,632 |
| 30 Acres winter barley | @ | 153 | | 4,590 |
| | | Total Farm Gross Margin | | 59,082 |

*Less* Fixed Costs:

| | | | |
|---|---|---|---|
| Labour | | 7,303 | |
| Power & Machinery – running costs | | 9,688 | |
| – replacement costs | | 5,744 (depreciation) | |
| Rent | | 6,400 | |
| Other costs | | 4,051 | 33,186 |
| | | Trading Margin | 25,896 |

*Less* Finance Costs:

| | | | |
|---|---|---|---|
| O/D interest | £600 | | |
| Loan capital & interest | £1,400 | | 2,000 |
| | | Margin | £23,896 |

available for drawings, taxation and further items of capital expenditure:

| | |
|---|---|
| New milking equipment March 1982 | £12,000 |
| Drawings | £5,000 |

The budget is based on *existing information and expected yield levels to be obtained*. The margin after finance costs of £23,896 should be compared with past performance detailed in audited accounts. It is certainly substantial. Also the individual gross margin levels stated can be checked against standard data (see Appendix 3), e.g. the dairy gross margin at £337 per cow is above average, but does not look too much out of line. However, the dairy replacement figure at £271 is high and could be questioned.

If you are sufficiently interested to re-work the whole budget using standard data (in Appendix 3) then Farmer A is about £9,000 above the average farmer on his trading margin figure.

*The main feature of the budget must be the margin of £23,896, which indicates that the borrowings of this farm business can easily be serviced.*

### 3. Summary of Farmer A

Here it is worth restating some of the main points:

*Farmer's Balance Sheet*

| | |
|---|---|
| Total assets | £113,376 |
| Liabilities | £18,050 |
| Net worth | £95,326 |
| Bank borrowing | £13,900 |

*Budget Margin:* £23,896.

*Rental Equivalent:* £26 per acre. As a percentage of gross output = 8%.

There should be no problems in this case!

Let us now look at another tenant farmer but in a *very* different situation:

### EXAMPLE FARMER B

No audited accounts are available and you have seen a lot of pressure on the bank account. When visiting the farm, a farmer's balance sheet is completed (see page 51–53).

**FARMER B**

FARMER'S BALANCE SHEET

NAME: FARMER B                      DATE: August 1981

BANK: X BANK

FARM ADDRESS: LITTLE VALLEY

FARM AREA

| | Owned | Tenanted |
|---|---|---|
| Crops | · | 80 |
| Grass | | 132 |
| Woodland and Roughland | | |
| Total | | 212 |

Rent Payable: £7,000

Landlord: A. Smith

ESTIMATED EFFECTIVE ACREAGE: 200

---

**Livestock**

Cattle *(Nos.)*

| | | | *(Market Value)*<br>£ | *Total Value*<br>£ |
|---|---|---|---|---|
| Dairy Cows | 80 | @ | 450 | 36,000 |
| Heifers | 25 | @ | 400 | 10,000 |
| Young Stock | 58 | @ | 150 | 8,700 |
| Pigs | | @ | | |
| | | @ | | |
| | | @ | | |
| Sheep | | @ | | |
| | | @ | | |
| | | @ | | |
| 3 Bulls | | @ | 1,000 | 3,000 |

Total £57,700

---

PRODUCE FOR OWN CONSUMPTION

| (Silage, Corn, Hay etc.) | | *Total Value*<br>£ |
|---|---|---|
| 60t. Corn | @ £100 per ton | 6,000 |
| 25t. Hay | @ £25 per ton | 625 |
| 110t. Silage | @ £16 per ton | 1,760 |
| | Total | £8,385 |

## FARMER B (Cont'd)

### Growing Crops

(value usually at cost of variable inputs only)

| Acres | Crop | £ | Total Value £ |
|-------|------|---|---------------|
| 80 | Winter barley | @ 37.50 | 2,790 |

### Stored Produce for Sale

| Crop | Tons | (Market value) | Total value |
|------|------|----------------|-------------|
| | | | Nil |

### Farm Machinery

| Date of purchase | Item | Cost £ | Market Value £ |
|------------------|------|--------|----------------|
| 1978 | 2 tractors | 2,000 | 6,000 |
| 1980 | 1 tractor | 7,000 | 7,000 |
| 1979 | milking equipment | 8,000 | 8,000 |
| Various other items | | | 11,900 |
| | | | 32,900 |

**FARMER B (Cont'd)**

| Liabilities | £ | Assets | £ |
|---|---|---|---|
| Rent outstanding | 5,100 | Cash at bank | — |
| Due to Bank | | Debtors | 2,100 |
| – Current Account | 70,830 | Grants due | — |
| – Loan Account | — | Stock | — |
| Creditors | 13,500 | – Produce for sale | |
| Hire Purchase | 1,600 | – Livestock | 57,700 |
| Private loans | | – Produce for own | 8,385 |
| (short-term) | — | consumption | |
| | | – Fertilizer/seed/feed etc. | 2,250 |
| | | Valuation | |
| | | – Growing crops | 2,970 |
| | | – Tenant right | 5,000 |
| Sub-total | 91,030 | Sub-total | 78,405 |
| Mortgages | | | — |
| Dilapidations | | Land & Buildings | 32,900 |
| Other Liabilities | | acres @ £ | — |
| Liabilities | 91,030 | Farm Machinery | |
| | | Tenant's improvements | |
| *Date* | | | |
| August 1981 | | | |
| **Net Worth/Balance** | 20,275 | | |
| | £111,305 | Total | £111,305 |

**Other Items:**

  1. Contingent liabilities:     Nil
  2. Leasing:             Nil
  3. Non-farming assets:      Nil

All this presents a dismal picture! Liabilities of £91,030 against total assets of £111,305. The net worth is only £20,275 and the farm machinery value at £32,900 could be questionable in the event of a forced sale. The gearing is very adverse and this farmer will have difficulty in servicing his borrowings. Also the creditor figure looks high.

**Rental equivalent**

| | |
|---|---|
| *Rent* | £7,000 |
| *Bank* O/D average balance (say) | |
| £55,000 @ 15% | £8,250 |
| Hire Purchase | £450 |
| | 15,700 ÷ effective acreage 200 |
| equals | £78 *per acre* (a high charge) |

**Rental equivalent as a percentage of output** (say, £62,488*)

$$\frac{15{,}700}{62{,}480} \times 100$$

$$= 25\% \text{ (a high charge)}$$

*Calculated from the sum of farm enterprise outputs

A farm budget is drawn up and reveals the following (see opposite).

**FARMER B**

### GROSS MARGIN BUDGET .

|  |  | Total |
|---|---|---|
|  | £ | £ |
| 80 Dairy cows @ | 280 | 22,400 |
| 25 Dairy replacements @ | 165 | 4,125 |
| 80 Acres winter barley @ | 122.5 | 9,920 |
| Farm Gross Margin | | 36,325 |

*Less* Fixed Costs

| Labour | 5,200 | |
|---|---|---|
| Power & machinery | | |
| running costs | 9,200 | |
| replacement costs | 4,850 | (depreciation) |
| Rent & rates | 7,000 | |
| Other costs | 3,100 | |
| | | 29,350 |
| Trading Margin | | £6,975 |

*Less* Finance Costs

| Bank interest | 8,250 | |
|---|---|---|
| H.P. & leasing | 450 | |
| | | 8,700 |
| Negative result = | | £1,725 |

*Before* drawings and other capital expenditure.

Clearly, Farmer B has severe problems. It looks as though he will continue to be unable to meet the financial commitments of the business. Looking at the budget – dairy performance and barley gross margin are low by average production standards. (See Appendix 3.) Farmer B must try to improve farm output, but will this be enough? I suspect not. Farmer B should consider making a capital injection to the business to restructure the borrowing to a level which can be serviced.

If there are no outside funds available, then, looking at the Farmers Balance

Sheet livestock section, the only other possibility is a stop-gap measure of selling the dairy followers (replacements) plus two of the bulls (why does he need three – one may well ask!) This would generate a badly needed £20,000. The dairy herd would continue to operate as a 'flying herd' which means replacements purchased only when necessary.

The rental equivalent would be reduced to £63 per acre. This is still high but Farmer B may be able to manage while endeavouring to increase farm output from his fresh starting point. Another £50 margin per cow would mean an extra £4,000 annual income from the herd of 80 cows.

## *EXAMPLE – FARMER C*

Here is another interesting situation: this time an owner-occupier of 242 acres (see opposite).

## FARMER C

| Liabilities | £ | Assets | £ |
|---|---|---|---|
| Rent outstanding | — | Cash at bank | — |
| Due to Bank | | Debtors | 500 |
| – Current Account | 84,510 | Grants due | — |
| – Loan Account | — | Stock | |
| Creditors | 5,000 | – Produce for sale | |
| Hire Purchase | — | – Livestock | 8,280 |
| Private Loans (short-term) | — | – Produce for own consumption | — |
| Sub Total | 89,510 | – Fertilizer/seed/feed etc. | 6,220 |
| Mortgages (AMC) | 70,100 | Valuation | |
| Dilapidations | — | – Growing Crops | 14,630 |
| Other Liabilities | — | – Tenant right | — |
| Liabilities | 159,610 | Sub Total | 29,630 |
| | | Land & Buildings | |
| | | 242 acres @ £1,500 | 363,000 |
| | | Farm Machinery | 29,300 |
| | | Tenant's improvements | — |
| Date | | | |
| **Net Worth/Balance** | 262,320 | | |
| | £421,930 | Total | £421,930 |

## Other Items:

1. Contingent liabilities:   Nil
2. Leasing:                  Nil
3. Non-farming assets: Life policy – surrender value £3,150

Looking at the Farmer's Balance Sheet, at first glance there would seem to be no problem.

| | |
|---|---|
| Total assets | £421,930 |
| Total liabilities | £159,610 |
| Net Worth | £262,320 |

However, this farmer, like Farmer B, is unable to service finance costs. His current liabilities far exceed his current assets. A farm budget reveals:

**Farm Gross Margin Budget**

| | | £ | £ |
|---|---|---|---|
| 200 Ewes | @  33.5 | 6,700 | |
| 90 Acres winter wheat | @ 185.5 | 16,700 | |
| 50 Acres winter barley | @ 153 | 7,680 | |
| 35 Acres winter oats | @ 167 | 5,845 | |
| Total Farm Gross Margins | | | 36,925 |

*Less* fixed costs:

| | | |
|---|---|---|
| Labour | 3,500 | |
| Farm machinery | | |
| – running | 6,900 | |
| – replacement | 5,210 (depreciation) | |
| Other costs | 6,080 | |
| | | 21,690 |
| Trading Margin | | 15,235 |

| | | |
|---|---|---|
| To meet finance costs: total | £21,700* | |
| plus drawings | £6,000 | |
| | | 27,700 |
| Negative Margin | | £12,465 |

*Rental Equivalent: £90 per acre*

*Rental Equivalent as % of Gross Output (say 57,500) = 37%*

*Bank O/D (say) £70,000 @ 15% £10,500
AMC (20 year loan)          £11,200

Farmer C is in a far stronger position in asset terms than Farmer B. He can sell a parcel of land to make a capital injection. However, before taking any action at all, I would suggest that this case needs some urgent attention by Farmer C's accountant.

Detailed profit and loss figures must be produced quickly to pinpoint the exact situation. Also, tax computations will need to be made to ascertain the amount of fixed assets to be sold or sold and leased back. It certainly looks as though some action is needed to reduce the financial burden. Farmer C is already above average in terms of farm output on his existing enterprises and improvements in this area will only have a minimal effect *unless* the farm enterprises can be *changed* to achieve significantly higher output, coupled with the same level of fixed costs or, better still, a lower level.

## 4. Break-even Analysis

The usual separation of farming costs into fixed and variable makes graphic presentation straightforward. In using break-even charts the link between variable costs and output is easily seen and the point of minimum output for the business to service its borrowing is also shown. (See example below.) This technique is useful on occasions when trying to illustrate the vulnerability of a particular farm business, i.e. when the margin of safety is slight or even non-existent.

This simple chart assumes an even spread of sales income over the year.

Farm Output                £60,000

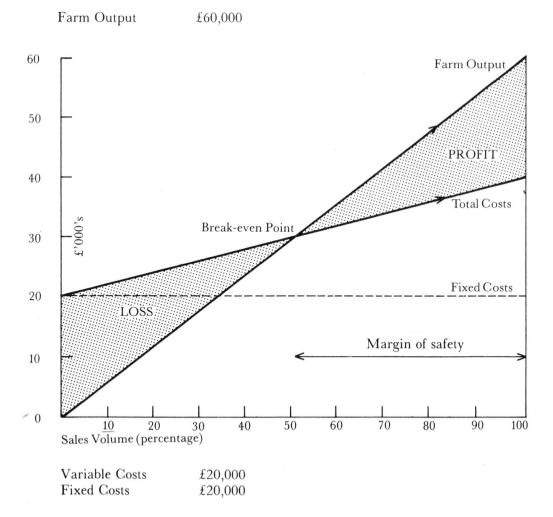

Variable Costs        £20,000
Fixed Costs           £20,000

In this case the break-even point is £30,000 farm output. There is a good margin of safety.

Alternatively break-even can be calculated arithmetically:

*as in our example*

| | |
|---|---|
| Farm output | £60,000 |
| *less* Variable cost | £20,000 |
| Farm gross margin | £40,000 |
| *less* Fixed costs | £20,000 |
| Trading margin | £20,000 |

As in our example

$$\text{Break-even output} = \text{fixed cost} \times \frac{\text{Farm output}}{\text{Farm gross margin}}$$

$$\text{Break-even} = 20,000 \times \frac{60,000}{40,000}$$

$$= £30,000$$

*Question*

At what level of output will the business achieve a trading margin of £40,000 – assuming fixed costs remain at the same level?

$$\text{New Output} = \text{Fixed costs} + \text{trading margin} \times \frac{\text{Output}}{\text{Farm gross margin}}$$

$$= 20,000 + 40,000 \times \frac{60,000}{40,000}$$

$$£90,000$$

## 5. Cash Flow Forecasts

The *profitability* of the farm business has been shown in the farm budget. The *viability* of the business in cash terms will be shown in the cash flow forecast. The basic principles of the cash flow forecast are exactly the same as with any other business. There are a few additional points to note:

  i The timing of many items is tied to biological and physical factors which may well be fixed (e.g. milk production – lactation period 44 weeks).

  ii If the cash flow forecast shows end of month positions – watch for 'pre milk-cheque overdraft peaks'. Milk cheques are usually dispatched by the Milk Marketing Board between the 18th and the 22nd monthly,

iii  Some farm enterprises extend over more than a 12 month period (e.g. 18 month beef), and again, harvest proceeds may not be received before farm input costs are being incurred for the next year's harvest.

iv  The farmer's technical plan as to the stocking and cropping of the farm is useful alongside the cash flow forecast to make sense of crop sales figures etc. (e.g. yield per acre × product price anticipated).

v  The farm business may well consist of several farm enterprises with differing cash flow forecast patterns, e.g.:

An *arable farm* will have peak requirements probably August to November before receipt of harvest proceeds.

*Dairy farms* generally show a lower requirement during the summer grazing months.

*Stock farms'* bank balances tend to peak in spring and autumn linking with livestock purchases/sales.

vi  If the cash flow negative peak balance is unacceptable – can it be restructured?

Sell crops/livestock earlier?

Buy farm inputs later?

Phase capital expenditure?

Use leasing of expensive machinery, instead of purchasing?

Use other farm input credit plans?

As with other businesses, high profit will be useless if there is no cash available for working capital – *there must be funds for the day to day running of the business.*

An abridged example of a farmer's cash flow forecast form is given on page 62 and guidance notes for the farmer on completing it on page 63.

# FARMER'S CASH FLOW FORECAST*

P = Planned        A = Actual

| Year | JAN. | | FEB. | | MAR. | | | ANNUAL SUMMARY | |
|---|---|---|---|---|---|---|---|---|---|
| | P | A | P | A | P | A | | P | A |
| *Income* | | | | | | | | | |
| Crops | | | | | | | | | |
| Livestock/Milk Sales | | | | | | | | | |
| Subsidies | | | | | | | | | |
| Other Income/Capital Introduced etc. | | | | | | | | | |
| TOTAL INCOME (A) | | | | | | | | | |
| *Payments* | | | | | | | | | |
| Variable Costs | | | | | | | | | |
| Fixed Costs | | | | | | | | | |
| Livestock Purchases | | | | | | | | | |
| Personal Drawings | | | | | | | | | |
| Other Expenditure | | | | | | | | | |
| TOTAL EXPENDITURE (B) | | | | | | | | | |
| MONTHLY BALANCE (A-B) (INITIAL BALANCE £00) | | | | | | | | | |
| CUMULATIVE BALANCE | | | | | | | | | |

*The complete form would have columns for 12 months plus the final annual summary

## Guidance Notes for the Farmer's Completion of the Cash Flow Forecast Form

1. Look at your farming enterprise plans for the coming 12 months and from these plans estimate your farm income and expenses. (Accepting that it is difficult to predict market prices and timing of sales.)
2. It will probably be useful to group your income under headings as follows: Crops; Livestock/Milk sales; Subsidies and any capital introduced.
3. Then group your expenses under headings as follows: Variable costs; fixed costs; livestock purchases; personal drawings; other expenditure.

| Examples of Variable Costs | Fixed Costs | Other Expenditure |
|---|---|---|
| Feeds. | Power & Machinery | Bank Charges. |
| Fertilizers. | running costs. | Mortgage repayment & |
| Spray. | Regular labour. | interest. |
| Vet. & Med. etc. | Rent & Rates. | Taxation. |
| | Building Repairs. | Capital expenditure (e.g. new |
| | Insurance – general. | tractor). |
| | Other costs. | |

4. Now total your income and expenses for each planned month and obtain a net *inflow* or *outflow* of cash.
5. Insert your starting bank balance and then progress forward through the months. You can now see clearly your predicted bank balances. (This will obviously be very useful for discussion with your Accountant and Bank Manager.)
6. You may now find the *peak* bank balance predicted unacceptably high. You could restructure this by, say altering the timing of your product sales; alter planned capital expenditure; merchant credit?; H.P. or Leasing?
7. *Finally* as the year progresses enter your *actual* income and expenses so that you compare your actuals with predictions.

## LOOKING AT THE BANK'S SECURITY

If you want 'comfort' in addition to the balance sheet net worth and in addition to the usual personal forms of security, the bank can take, in the case of the *owner occupier,* a first or second charge on the farm deeds. In the case of the *tenant farmer* you may take an agricultural charge or sometimes obtain an Agricultural Credit Corporation (ACC) guarantee.

The Agricultural Credits Act 1928 enables a bank to take a charge on a tenant farmer's live and dead stock and other farming assets. Most banks have a special charge form. This is effectively a mortgage similar to a debenture issued by a limited company. The agricultural charge enables a bank to appoint a receiver, if necessary, to take over the farming assets and liquidate the business to recover the bank's money.

An ACC guarantee is available to tenant farmers in certain situations of farm development. The Corporation supply a guarantee to the farmer's bank to support the bank facility made available at the commencement of the farm development programme. (See Chapter 5 for further details.)

### Conclusion on Assessment Methods

We have looked at several techniques useful in assessing the agricultural proposition. Personally, I still think that the dominant factor is the farmer himself. Sophisticated farm planning techniques will help but will never achieve anything unless the farmer himself is a capable businessman.

You should by now have formed a mental picture of the two main farm finance assessment 'keys':

### ASSET COVER and SERVICEABILITY

You will find some businesses with both good asset cover and serviceability; some with one and not the other, and some farm businesses with neither!

To conclude this chapter, the following is offered as a specimen letter to control setting out a farm lending position. A checklist to use in reviewing farm business finance is given in Appendix 10.

## SPECIMEN LETTER TO CONTROL

### Re: Farmer Checkley

I visited Checkley's farm last Friday (2.2.82) at West Chiltington and now enclose an Application for Funds for £60,000 on overdraft and £70,000 on loan repayable at £12,000 per annum.

*The Farm and Enterprises*

The farm extends to 500 acres of which 200 acres are owned and 300 acres rented at £30 per acre. The land is mainly average grade 3 (MAFF classification old system) but there are some fields possibly grade 2 with good cereal growing potential.

The farm is run by Checkley, his wife and two full-time men. They are all fully employed looking after the Dairy Herd of 120 Friesian Cows with followers and the 300 acres of cereals. The remaining land is down to grass to support the Dairy Herd and followers.

Overall the farm looks, as always, in good shape and the Dairy Herd are performing well with an average milk yield of over 1100 gallons per cow per annum. (See Milk Marketing Board figures enclosed.)

The cereals are all winter sown and look well established. Yields last harvest were around 2 tons per acre which is good for this area of the County.

The farm buildings and machinery are adequate at present for the farm systems being operated.

*Financial Data*

(i) *Audited Accounts*

I enclose the last 3 years balance sheets and accounts from which I have extracted the following:

| Year end | 31/3/79 | 31/3/80 | 31/3/81 |
|---|---|---|---|
| Profit | £8,120 | 7,285 | 10,250 |
| after depreciation | 5,250 | 6,700 | 7,250 |
| Drawings | 2,500 | 8,000 | 3,500 |
| Capital | £50,120 | £54,160 | £62,500 |

You will note the steady record of profitability.

(ii) *Farmer's Balance Sheet*

This was completed by Farmer Checkley at the completion of my farm visit (2/2/82) and by using up-to-date realistic market valuations for livestock and land shows a net worth (capital) of £454,080. This is due mainly to the land owned, 200 acres @ £1,500 per acre and the Dairy Herd at £500 per cow.

(In the Audited Accounts the Dairy Cows are treated on a 'herd basis' and valued at only £150 per cow, and the land is substantially undervalued.)
The total debts are stated at £61,545 which includes trade creditors at £11,160 representing 6 weeks normal credit.

## The Proposal

The opportunity has arisen for Checkley to purchase an adjoining plot of land (70 acres) which he rents at the moment.

The price will be acceptable at £84,000 (£1,200 per acre) and Checkley believes it feasible to repay a loan of £70,000 at £12,000 per annum.

The local Ministry man (ADAS section) has been to the farm and helped prepare a Cash Flow Forecast and Farm Budget to demonstrate feasibility (see enclosed).

The Cash Flow Forecast shows a peak requirement of £58,050 just before harvest and the Farm Budget shows a projected margin of £2,520 after finance charges and drawings. The rental equivalent is £54 per acre; although a little high, Checkley should manage this figure.

## Recommendation

Land purchase is of course difficult to fund these days with land prices far outweighing earning capacity.

However, in view of Checkley's good track record, the farm held as security and the demonstrated project viability I recommend support.


(signed)
A A BRANCH MANAGER


Suggested enclosures:

    (i)  Application for Funds form
  (ii)  Milk Marketing Board records
 (iii)  3 years' Audited Accounts
 (iv)  Farmer's Balance Sheet (2.2.82)
  (v)  Cash Flow Forecast
 (vi)  Farm Budget

CHAPTER 5

# Sources of Finance

Taking a view of the UK Farming Balance Sheet the industry looks very healthy financially. The ratio of net worth to borrowed funds is high.

### LIABILITIES

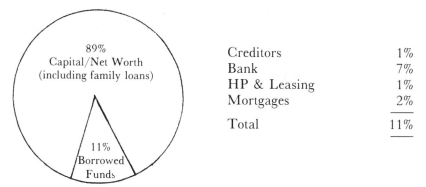

| | |
|---|---|
| Creditors | 1% |
| Bank | 7% |
| HP & Leasing | 1% |
| Mortgages | 2% |
| Total | 11% |

The balance sheet is very strong because of the substantial value of land and buildings representing 72% of total assets.

### ASSETS

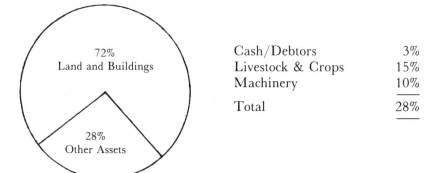

| | |
|---|---|
| Cash/Debtors | 3% |
| Livestock & Crops | 15% |
| Machinery | 10% |
| Total | 28% |

## Principal Sources of Finance

For *long-term finance* (over 7 years) for e.g. land purchase, long-term building improvements, drainage, the alternative sources of finance could be *bank loan, Agricultural Mortgage Corporation, private loans, insurance companies.*

For the *medium-term* (5–7 years) for e.g. land improvement schemes, breeding herds, short-life buildings, machinery, the farmer could look to: *bank loan, hire-purchase, leasing, machinery syndicate schemes.*

For the *short-term,* for normal working capital, stock purchases, bridging finance, fertilisers, sprays, etc., there could be: *bank overdraft, point of sale credit (e.g. input finance schemes), merchants' credit, leasing.*

Whilst the banks provide the major amount of finance by way of overdraft, short- or medium-term loans, land purchase loans and business loans, there are many other sources of finance. The principle ones are reviewed in this chapter.

## TRADE CREDITS

This is an important source of credit to the farmer, provided mainly by general agricultural merchants. Although this may carry the penalty of higher interest rates and a loss of discount which would normally have been obtained through bulk purchases, traditionally it is an easy source of credit as it does not involve lengthy interviews with the bank manager!

Merchants have in the past taken a tolerant attitude to the farmer and if the harvest is unsufficient to meet the outstanding seed, fertilizer and feed bill then the merchant has carried the outstanding balance forward. However, merchants are now becoming concerned at the cost of this ever increasing funding of the farmer and this has led to the development of Point of Sale Credit Schemes through the banks' subsidiary companies (See below).

### POINT OF SALE CREDIT

This would normally be arranged through one of the banks' subsidiary companies. Usually linked to an Agricultural Merchant Scheme, the finance is available to cover farming input costs, e.g. fertilizer, seed, feed etc. Loans are available on an unsecured basis at a fixed or floating interest rate option. Also, machinery loans can be arranged through machinery dealer schemes, again at fixed or floating rate options.

Trends indicate that the use of point of sale finance by farmers has increased in recent years. We may consider some of the reasons why this has occurred:

  i Subsidised sales aid schemes promoted by manufacturers and machinery distributors at low interest rates are attractive to farmers. Farmers who have never needed to borrow find these schemes hard to refuse.

  ii Due to increasing economic pressure the need to maintain and increase productivity by prudent investment has meant that each purchasing decision has become increasingly a financial decision. Manufacturers and distributors have therefore realised that offering the farmer a financial package increases the opportunity of a successful sale.

iii Due to the dual effect of inflation and the recession many more farmers are in the position of needing to borrow to maintain the efficiency of their enterprises. For many it is more convenient to take advantage of point of sale finance which is made available to them on the farm than to disturb their existing financial arrangements.

One indicator that confirms the increase of point of sale finance is the tractor market. During recent years, whilst the sale of new registered units has fallen the actual percentage sold using point of sale finance facilities has risen from 21% to 37%. One of the more popular point of sale facilities is leasing

## LEASING

This can provide an attractive alternative to the outright purchase of expensive machinery and equipment if the farming enterprise is unable to obtain full tax advantages in respect of capital allowances.

The basic concept of leasing is that it separates ownership from the use of the equipment. The farmer leasing a machine enjoys all the benefits from use of that machine, while ownership remains with the leasing company. In consideration for the arrangement the farmer pays a rental.

The most common forms of leasing in agriculture are:

*Plant Hire:* Normally very short term hire of large items of machinery, e.g. contractors plant etc.

*Financial Lease:* Often termed the full payout lease. The amount borrowed to fund the equipment is repaid plus an element of interest over an agreed period of time.

*Contract Hire:* Similar to the financial lease, but with the important difference that the resale proceeds of the machine at the end of the contract constitutes the final rental.

Of the three types of leasing the financial lease is the most prevalent.

The financial lease is a contract whereby the amount advanced to pay for the equipment is repaid, together with an element of interest, over an agreed time period known as the primary period. After the primary period continued use of the machine is available on payment of a nominal rental. The farmer never owns the machine but on eventual sale he receives the resale proceeds by way of a rebate of rentals. The farmer is responsible for the operating costs and it is in his own interest to ensure the machine is well maintained as he will benefit from an enhanced resale price as a result of good condition.

A contract hire agreement is similar but the rentals paid during the primary period are less because the resale proceeds at the end of the period belong to the leasing company. Continued use of the machine after the end of the primary period is not possible, and it is usual to replace the machine with another on contract hire. Sometimes contract hire arrangements include a provision for full maintenance costs during the primary period.

## The Benefits of Leasing

*Cashflow*
One of the major benefits of leasing is that it places no large immediate demand on farm cashflow when the machine is acquired. The rental payments will be made out of future income. This means working capital can be released for deployment in other parts of the farm business.

*Cost of Finance*
Unlike other forms of finance, lease rentals are fully allowable against tax, the whole of the rental is allowable not just the interest element. The farmer loses the capital allowance on the equipment as he is not, and never will be, the owner. This can of course be a major advantage, depending on his tax situation, as the lease rentals will reflect some of the benefits which the leasing company gains from claiming the capital allowances.

Where the marginal tax rate is no more than 30% the cost of leasing is competitive with other forms of finance, even with a tax rate in excess of 30% it can still be attractive for several reasons such as cashflow and cost etc. Where no tax is being paid then leasing will normally be the cheapest method of finance as the capital allowances will be of no value to the farmer.

*Certainty of Arrangement*
A leasing agreement is a fixed contract and cannot be withdrawn early unless default occurs in payment of the rentals. It therefore protects the farmer from future economic changes or credit-squeeze situations. The leasing company is unable to amend the basic terms of the lease once negotiated and therefore cannot alter or accelerate rentals once they have been agreed.

*Ease of Budgeting*
Due to the regular nature of the payment of rentals, leasing makes forward budgeting much easier. It also highlights the cost of a machine in terms of what income it must generate to justify its acquisition.

*Flexibility*
Farming is by its nature a seasonal business which dictates its own buying and selling patterns. Farm enterprises also have different cashflows and few farms, apart from intensive dairy, can claim a regular monthly pattern of income and expenditure. The rental structure of the primary period of a lease can be constructed to fit the income and expenditure pattern of the farm. (For comparative costs of a lease/bank loan, see table opposite.)

## HIRE PURCHASE

Mainly used for items of machinery. Generally more expensive than other lines of credit but has the advantage of ownership passing to the farmer on completion of the hire-purchase payments. This can be appropriate where grants are involved.

**Comparison of Cost of Financing a Machine**

Machine Cost: £10,000     Accounting Year End: 31 March
Funding Term: 3 years     Machine Acquired: 1 April

*Marginal Tax Rate 30%*

| | LEASE | | | BANK LOAN | | |
|---|---|---|---|---|---|---|
| | Rentals: £98.8 per quarterly in advance | £1000 | | Capital: Equal quarterly repayments | | |
| | | | | Interest: 17% on outstanding capital balance | | |
| | *Rentals* | *Tax Benefit*[1] | *Net Cost* | *Repayments* | *Tax Benefit*[2] | *Net Cost* |
| YEAR 1 | 3,952 | — | 3,952 | 4,810 | — | 4,810 |
| YEAR 2 | 3,952 | (1,186) | 2,766 | 4,240 | (3,440) | 794 |
| YEAR 3 | 3,952 | (1,186) | 2,766 | 3,720 | (276) | 3,444 |
| YEAR 4 | — | (1,186) | (1,186) | — | (108) | (108) |
| TOTAL | 11,856 | (3,558) | 8,298 | 12,770 | (3,830) | 8,940 |

*Notes:*
1 Lease rentals are a trading expense and therefore reduce income tax repayable.
2 The interest element of the bank loan repayments is a trading expense and therefore reduces income tax payable.
   A first year allowance of 100% has been taken.

**Equipment Leasing in UK Agriculture**

The use of leasing facilities by farmers has also grown very significantly in the last few years. In terms of the total investment in plant and machinery the share which leasing has taken has been steadily increasing.

| | | *1977* | *1978* | *1979* | *1980* |
|---|---|---|---|---|---|
| Investment in plant, machinery & vehicles[1] | £m | 514 | 582 | 629 | 547 |
| Leasing[2] | £m | 31 | 38 | 78 | 81 |
| Leasing as % of total | | 6.0% | 6.5% | 12.4% | 14.8% |

*Notes:*
1 Source – *Annual Review of Agriculture 1981.*
2 Equipment Leasing Association statistics adjusted.

## SYNDICATE CREDIT

Farmers who are prepared to co-operate in buying and using machinery can do this through syndicates organised by National Farmers Union. The banks will advance a high proportion of the purchase cost, usually around 80%. This system is often used for example to purchase expensive pea vining equipment used in the Eastern counties. Fixed costs to each farmer are therefore reduced through joint ownership which helps the liquidity situation on the individual farms.

Bank financing is usually flexible and competitive. The syndicate may consist of two to twenty NFU members and repayment of finance can be up to seven years. Although new or second-hand machinery may be purchased most syndicates tend to buy new machinery.

Syndication can thus give the farmer access to machinery that he might not otherwise have been able to afford. As regards taxation, the same depreciation allowances are available – the individual farmer takes his share of allowance in the same proportion as his syndicate share. To apply for a loan farmers will approach a bank through their local NFU Secretary.

## INSURANCE COMPANIES

Some insurance companies will make mortgage advances on farms and estates at interest rates reflecting market conditions. The repayment of such loans is usually linked to an endowment policy.

## PRIVATE LOANS

Traditionally a common source of finance from relatives. The advantages usually are that the rate of interest is below the current market rate and also that repayments tend to be on a very flexible basis.

## AGRICULTURAL CREDIT CORPORATION (ACC)

The function of the corporation is to help the efficient and progressive farmer obtain bank credit. This is achieved by guaranteeing the bank borrowing which the farmer may require for a wide range of operations. There is a charge for this service and the current annual fee is 2½% of the sum guaranteed* but this can vary depending on the circumstances of each case. The fee of course reduces as the bank limit and guarantee are reduced during the repayment programme. The bank thus obtains the benefits of the security provided by the ACC guarantee and the farmer obtains the bank borrowing he requires to implement his development programme.

The corporation was formed in 1959 sponsored by the National Farmers Union as it was considered that agricultural credit was difficult to obtain for medium-term finance – particularly for the young progressive farmer. The corporation was set up in its present form in 1964 and received government support under the provisions of the Agriculture and Horticulture Act 1964 and the Agriculture Act 1967. It operates throughout the UK.

An ACC guarantee can benefit both the bank and the farmer: the bank obtains the benefit of ACC's technical and financial assessment of the development programme together with the security provided by the guarantee: the farmer obtains

---

*This is a guide rate only. ACC are flexible with regard to rates.

the bank borrowing he requires to implement the development programme, enabling him to progress more rapidly than would otherwise be possible.

To apply for finance the applicant, either independently or with the help of his adviser or bank manager, completes the application forms available from ACC and forwards them to the Corporation together with his development plans, supporting budgets and past accounts. After initial appraisal, a member of ACC's technical staff visits the holding to discuss the proposal in greater detail.

If the applicant is successful, ACC offers a guarantee to the bank and negotiates the required credit facilities. ACC then writes to the applicant setting out the terms and conditions of its offer of guarantee and the formalities to be completed.

ACC then signs the guarantee and the bank facility is made available so that the development programme may begin.

After the guarantee has been signed, ACC needs to be kept informed of progress in the business. The situation is reviewed at least once a year when the farmer must provide an up-to-date statement of assets and liabilities and his latest accounts. ACC staff are available to discuss any problems that may arise in implementing the development programme and a member visits the holding annually or as required to review progress.

ACC guarantees to repay the bank borrowing if the farmer fails to do so and this enables the bank to lend in circumstances where adequate security is not otherwise available. The farmer, however, always retains the ultimate responsibility for repaying the debt.

Farmers, growers and co-operatives can apply whether they are owner-occupiers, tenants or potential new entrants into the industry. The scheme is particularly applicable to tenants who find they have often insufficient alternative security to offer to their bank.

As regards eligibility – creditworthy farmers and growers who have viable development plans may apply. The applicant's past experience and present capital position are taken into account in assessing the potential profitability of the programme and his ability to service and repay the borrowing within a reasonable period.

Most medium-term expenditure, including purchase of farm and horticultural buildings, fixed plant, machinery and equipment, livestock and working capital can be financed in this way.

Circumstances in which a guarantee might be appropriate:

(a) Expansion of existing business. The guarantee may permit expansion to be undertaken in one significant step as opposed to slower development geared to a build-up in capital.
(b) An increase in the size of the present holding or a proposed move to a larger one.
(c) A new entrant into the industry. Banks may feel unable to help a new entrant due to the lack of any record of his ability to run a successful business.
(d) The replacement of other security such as a personal guarantee.
(e) The purchase of part of the existing business from partners or other beneficiaries under a will.

(f) Paying off existing high interest rate sources of borrowing if the business is basically sound.

(g) A co-operative marketing development. The capital structure and underlying assets are sometimes insufficient in a new or expanding co-operative to satisfy the banks until a successful record has been established. A special scheme designed to help in these cases provides guarantees for advance payments and/or capital investment projects.

*Flexibility:* ACC's policy is to interfere as little as possible while bank repayments are being made satisfactorily. If problems arise, ACC examines the position with the farmer and his bank manager and consideration can be given to rephasing the repayment programme. Where further development appears worthwhile, a new guarantee for a higher sum can be considered. ACC staff are agriculturalists who appreciate the problems of the industry and its financial requirements will be considered sympathetically.

ACC combines the advantages of independent operation and Government support which means the guarantee facility can be provided at minimum cost. It opens up the possibility of new or increased borrowing. The additional cost of the guarantee is small considering the dual advantage of cheaper credit and a longer, more flexible repayment programme.

*Free* guarantees can also be made available to co-operatives undertaking a new marketing project through a scheme which is jointly organised by ACC* and the Central Council for Agricultural and Horticultural Co-operation (see Chapter 6).

## AGRICULTURAL MORTGAGE CORPORATION P.L.C.

The AMC was incorporated in 1928. The shareholders are: Bank of England; Barclays; Lloyds; Midland; National Westminster; Williams & Glyns, and assets currently exceed £400m. Operating under the provisions of the Agricultural Credits Acts 1928 and 1932, AMC normally grants loans for periods of between 5 and 40 years at a fixed or variable rate of interest.

Loans may be used for any agricultural purpose including:

purchase of farm property;
repayment of other borrowing;
capital improvements;
provision of working capital.

Decisions in principle can be given within 24 hours provided that all necessary information is supplied. Funds are readily available allowing AMC to offer a wide and flexible choice of borrowing facilities. AMC makes no charge for the consideration of applications for granting loans, provided that any loan offer is taken up.

AMC loans cannot be called in provided the borrower observes the obligations of the mortgage deed. Instalments are paid half-yearly but arrangements can be

*The ACC address is: 25–31 Knightsbridge, London SW1X 7NJ. Telephone No. 01 235 6292. CCAHC address is: 301–344 Market Towers, New Covent Market, 19 Elms Lane, London SW8 5NQ. Telephone No. 01 720 2144.

made to pay monthly if required. In the event of a borrower's death, a loan is not subject to recall.

## Types of Loan

*Repayment* – from 5 to 40 years, with a choice of repayment methods, the maximum amount advanced being two-thirds of the value of the security offered, as certified by AMC's valuer.

*Repayment* – from 5 to 40 years, the capital being repaid at the end of the period, the maximum loan being limited to one half of the value of the security.

## Interest Rates

All types of loan are available at fixed or variable rates of interest or any combination of the two. *Loans at fixed rate* will bear interest throughout the term at the rate ruling on the date of completion of the loan. *Loans at variable rate* initially bear interest at the rate ruling at completion, but are subject to quarterly review on the 1st day of March, June, September and December.

*Conversion Option* – variable rate borrowers may convert all or part of their loans to fixed rate at any time free of charge. Because of its long-term funding commitments, AMC is not prepared to convert fixed rate loans to a variable interest basis or to a lower fixed rate.

## Lending Criteria

Before a loan can be offered; AMC needs to be satisfied that:

>   the property offered represents adequate security for the loan, usually a complete agricultural unit although in some cases AMC is prepared to offer a loan on bare land;
>   the applicant has sufficient capital resources to carry out his proposals;
>   the farming will be carried out by a suitably experienced person;
>   although there is no minimum acreage requirement, the overall farming business is capable of providing an adequate livelihood after servicing all borrowing commitments, both from AMC and other sources.

*Let properties* – loans may be granted to landlords on let property depending upon the circumstances.

*Intensive units* (such as horticulture, pig or poultry enterprises) – loans on this type of property will usually be restricted to a maximum of 10 years and to 50% of the valuation and must be repaid by the annuity or endowment assurance methods.

## Methods of Repayment

Repayments may be by one or a combination of the following methods, although AMC will always consider other proposals to meet individual requirements.

*Annuity* – Half yearly payments comprising both interest and capital. The interest portion only ranks for tax relief and in the early years this forms the bulk of the instalment.

*Endowment assurance* – Half yearly payments comprising interest only to AMC on the total sum advanced and the premiums payable to the Life Office concerned on an endowment assurance policy to provide for the repayment of the loan. Tax relief is allowable on the interest payment and on such proportion of the premiums as laid down by the Inland Revenue.

AMC will require the assignment of a suitable endowment assurance policy owned by an adult on a life in which there is an insurable interest with the maturity date coinciding with the term of loan offered.

*A 'minimum cover' with-profits policy* is acceptable if designed to achieve a maturity value sufficient to repay the loan by the end of the term. Annual or intermediate bonuses only are taken into account. Terminal bonuses should be ignored.

Borrowers are free to choose the Life Office and type of policy to suit their particular needs subject to AMC's approval. Policies written under the Married Women's Property Acts or subject to a trust are not acceptable to AMC.

In the event of the maturity value proving insufficient the repay the loan in full at the end of the term, any balance would then become legally repayable, but AMC would be willing to accept any reasonable arrangement for the repayment of such balance over a suitable term. The basic information required at the outset should be supplied by the insurance company of the applicant's choice on form AMC.542 available from AMC on request.

It is always possible at modest cost to change to another repayment method, if, at the time, this offers an advantage to the borrower. In some cases an amendment to the lending rate of interest may be necessary. The interest due is notified annually by AMC to the local Inspector of Taxes. Relief appropriate to the tax situation of the borrower and/or his farming business is normally obtainable.

The endowment assurance method usually gives a borrower with sufficient liability for tax a greater measure of relief. The gross (before tax) cost of servicing a loan on this basis is invariably greater than on the annuity method. In considering the net (after tax) cost on an endowment basis with that of any other, borrowers must make their own assessment of the value to them of having their loan arrangements linked with life assurance.

Consultation with an accountant is recommended before making a choice of repayment method.

### How to Apply

Applications for loans should be made on forms AMC.1 and 27 and should be accompanied by the following:

    copies of the applicant's farming accounts for the last three years for the confidential information of AMC and its valuer;
    forward budgets for the next two years' farming operations (AMC637);
    a schedule of the Ordnance Survey Numbers and Areas together with an exact plan of the property offered as security;
    sale particulars where appropriate.

## Facilities Available to Existing Borrowers

Further loans are always available subject to AMC's lending criteria, the current valuation of the existing property and any additional security, if offered. The rate of interest on the further loan will be that ruling on the date it is completed. The rate of interest and conditions applying to existing loans will not be affected in any way.

## Sales of Mortgaged Property

Where the whole of the property is to be sold – subject to AMC's lending criteria, borrowers have the choice of:

taking the loan with them to be secured on another farm at the same rate of interest, in which case no charge is made by AMC;
transferring the loan to an approved purchaser of the security property, subject to a fee which will be quoted on request:
repaying the loan in full.

Where part only is to be sold AMC will co-operate in releasing a portion of the land charged, provided that the remainder can still be regarded as adequate security, subject to any necessary adjustment of the loan and payment of a fee which in most cases will be small.

*Early Repayment* – although borrowers have no legal right to repay a loan other than by the method set out in the mortgage deed, AMC is prepared to consider earlier repayment on terms to be quoted at the time of the request. In the case of a fixed interest rate loan, a fee not exceeding any loss occasioned to AMC by the repayment will be payable. It should be appreciated that, in certain circumstances, this fee might be substantial but where the repayment does not involve AMC in a loss the fee will be nominal. As regards a variable interest rate loan, no redemption fee is charged by AMC.*

## GOVERNMENT GRANTS

Basically there are two main schemes – the Agricultural and Horticultural Development Scheme (AHDS) which replaced the Farm and Horticultural Development Scheme and came into operation on 1 October 1980. The second scheme is the Argicultural and Horticultural Grant Scheme (AHGS) which came into operation on 1 October 1980, superceding the Farm Capital Grant Scheme and the Horticultural Capital Grant Scheme.

Details of both schemes are complex and the farmer is best advised to refer to his local office of the Ministry of Agriculture.

*The address of AMC is: Bucklersbury House, Queen Victoria Street, London, EC4N 8DU. Telephone No. 01-236 5252.

## AHDS (Agricultural and Horticultural Development Scheme)

The object of the scheme is to help established agricultural and horticultural businesses to modernise and so to increase their income above a certain level. Rates of grant vary from 5% for plant and machinery to 50% for field drainage. There are special rates available for less favourable agricultural areas.

A Farm Development Plan Example is given in Appendix 11.

## AHGS (Agricultural and Horticultural Grant Scheme)

Grants are payable on expenditure of a capital nature incurred in the carrying out or establishment of an agricultural or horticultural business. Rates vary from 15% to 37½% with less favoured areas again qualifying for special higher rates.

## SALE AND LEASEBACK

This is a way of releasing capital. By entering a sale and leaseback agreement an owner-occupier will sell the farm to a pension fund or other institution while carrying on farming as a tenant. Cash is then available to expand the farm business or take on additional land. The cost of such a deal should be carefully looked at by the farmer and his accountant – there will be taxation implications as well as a loss of capital value. For example, where the vacant possession sale value is say £1,600 per acre, on a sale and leaseback the value will probably be only 60% (£960 per acre).

Capital gains tax rules will apply if the farmer makes a capital gain on the sale. However, 'roll-over relief' can be obtained by planned reinvestment of the proceeds. This calls for advice from an accountant.

A rent of 3½/4% will be looked for by the new owners. On a value of say £960 per acre, this will mean £33–£38 per acre. Pension fund managers for example will be looking for the best possible return and rent reviews will be likely every three years.

## FOREIGN CURRENCY LOANS

In 1980/81 the Swiss banks in London were receiving many enquiries from farmers as to the methods of borrowing money abroad at cheaper rates. To take *full advantage* the farmer has to accept the *full risk of foreign exchange movements* in the same way as any other type of business borrowing funds by this means. I usually make the following points to farmers:

(a) If a farmer has no matching foreign currency receipts which he can utilise to repay the foreign currency borrowing, then he will be facing an open-ended foreign exchange exposure. That is to say, he will be committed to repay the foreign currency borrowing at some date in the future and will not know (unless he enters into a foreign exchange contract) how much this will cost him in sterling terms.

(b) If the farmer wishes to fix the total sterling cost of his foreign currency borrowing at the outset, then he can buy forward the necessary foreign currency. However, looking at the foreign exchange market, currencies which are cheaper to borrow in than sterling are naturally at a forward premium to sterling. Therefore, if you add the forward premium to the interest costs the resultant total cost of borrowing foreign currency and covering forward will virtually equal the cost of borrowing sterling. For example, looking at rates in the *Financial Times,* on the Euro Currency interest rate market, borrowing in Swiss francs is definitely the cheapest at the time of writing. Rates are quoted for three months at 8¼% to 8⅜%. However, you must then add on the premium for forward cover which equates to 5.03% per annum in the case of a Swiss currency borrowing. The bank would additionally charge an 'interest turn' and therefore the true rate of borrowing would be in the region of 15% to 16%.

(c) There have been many instances in the recent past where appreciation of the Swiss franc against sterling has more than off-set any initial interest rate advantage.

(d) There is also a possible taxation problem in that foreign exchange losses realised on repayment of currency loans which are related to capital transactions may not be allowable for tax in a general farming trading situation.

## RETURN ON CAPITAL

As stated earlier farming gives a low return on assets employed particularly in the owner-occupier situation as the land value far outweighs the earning capacity. Recalling figures from Chapter 4, the average of *tenants assets* per acre will be around £400 and the return, before interest charges and tax, between 10% (average) to 15% (premium). Let us compare the tenant farmer's return with that of the owner-occupier.

**Tenant Farmer**

say 300 acres @ £400 per acre
Total assets £120,000
Return:

| *Average* | *Premium* |
|---|---|
| 10% | 15% |
| £40 per acre | £60 per acre |
|   (or £12,000 per annum) |   (or £18,000 per annum) |

**Owner-occupier**

Taking the same farm but in an owner-occupier situation we must include land value, average £1,600 per acre.

Total assets are now 300 acres @ £2,000 per acre = *£600,000* and the return falls drastically to 2.75% (average) to 3.75% (premium).
Return:

| *Average* | *Premium* |
|---|---|
| 2.75% | 3.75% |
| £55 per acre | £75 per acre |
|   (or £16,500 per annum) |   (or £22,500 per annum) |

Although the return is very low on a land investment basis, the compensating factor has been the substantial increase in land values over the years. *Land prices averaged £130 per acre in 1961.*

The following table is a summary of figures from the Ministry of Agriculture Survey of Farm Incomes – 1980/81 and shows the average tenant's capital per acre and the return on an average farm.

| Farm Type | Tenants' Capital per acre | Return |
|---|---|---|
| Specialist dairy | £512 | 12% |
| Mainly dairy | £366 | 10% |
| Cattle & sheep | | |
| Upland | £122 | 10% |
| Lowland | £295 | 4.5% |
| Crops, cattle & sheep | £297 | 6.3% |
| Specialist cereals | £275 | 11% |
| General cropping | £338 | 11% |
| Pigs & poultry | £616 | 15% |
| *Average* of the EIGHT | £353 | 10% |

Further details for each of the eight types of farm (total farm output/inputs, net income etc.) are shown on the following pages. The figures given are general guidelines.

# RETURN ON CAPITAL FOR VARIOUS FARM TYPES

| **Specialist Dairy** | *1979/80* | *1980/81* |
|---|---|---|
| Average Size of Farm | 121 Acres | 123 Acres |
| | £ | £ |
| Total Farm Output | 47,091 | 52,858 |
| Total Farm Inputs | 40,505 | 45,152 |
| Net Farm Income | 6,586 | 7,707 |
| Average Tenant's Capital | 57,190 | 62,972 |
| (per acre) | (£473) | (£512) |
| *Return on Capital* | 11% | 12% |

| **Mainly Dairy** | | |
|---|---|---|
| Average Size of Farm | 262 Acres | 264 Acres |
| | £ | £ |
| Total Farm Output | 68,694 | 76,244 |
| Total Farm Inputs | 59,864 | 66,485 |
| Net Farm Income | 8,830 | 9,760 |
| Average Tenant's capital | 88,334 | 96,687 |
| (per acre) | (£337) | (£366) |
| *Return on Capital* | 10% | 10% |

| **Cattle and Sheep (Upland)** | *1979/80* | *1980/81* |
|---|---|---|
| Average Size of Farm | 521 Acres | 524 Acres |
| | £ | £ |
| Total Farm Output | 28,539 | 33,017 |
| Total Farm Inputs | 24,169 | 26,900 |
| Net Farm Income | 4,370 | 6,117 |
| Average Tenant's Capital | 59,765 | 63,686 |
| (per acre) | (£115) | (£122) |
| *Return on Capital* | 7% | 10% |

|                          | *1979/80*   | *1980/81*   |
|--------------------------|-------------|-------------|
| **Cattle and Sheep (Lowland)** |       |             |
| Average Size of Farm     | 158 Acres   | 158 Acres   |
|                          | £           | £           |
| Total Farm Output        | 22,659      | 25,890      |
| Total Farm Inputs        | 21,810      | 23,821      |
| Net Farm Income          | 850         | 2,069       |
| Average Tenant's Capital | 43,479      | 46,536      |
| (per acre)               | (£275)      | (£295)      |
| *Return on Capital*      | 2%          | 4.5%        |

| **Crops, Cattle and Sheep** |          |             |
|--------------------------|-------------|-------------|
| Average Size of Farm     | 216 Acres   | 214 Acres   |
|                          | £           | £           |
| Total Farm Output        | 40,257      | 43,545      |
| Total Farm Inputs        | 35,375      | 39,502      |
| Net Farm Income          | 4,882       | 4,042       |
| Average Tenant's Capital | 59,069      | 63,683      |
| (per acre)               | (£273)      | (£297)      |
| *Return on Capital*      | 8.2%        | 6.3%        |

| **Specisalist Cereals**  |             |             |
|--------------------------|-------------|-------------|
| Average Size of Farm     | 298 Acres   | 300 Acres   |
|                          | £           | £           |
| Total Farm Output        | 54,395      | 62,288      |
| Total Farm Inputs        | 47,349      | 53,126      |
| Net Farm Income          | 7,045       | 9,162       |
| Average Tenant's Capital | 74,730      | 82,601      |
| (per acre)               | (£250)      | (£275)      |
| *Return on Capital*      | 9%          | 11%         |

|                          | *1979/80* | *1980/81* |
|--------------------------|-----------|-----------|
| **General Cropping**     |           |           |
| Average Size of Farm     | 278 Acres | 280 Acres |
|                          | £         | £         |
| Total Farm Output        | 79,132    | 84,809    |
| Total Farm Inputs        | 65,604    | 47,641    |
| Net Farm Income          | 13,528    | 10,168    |
| Average Tenant's Capital | 85,511    | 94,569    |
| (per acre)               | (£308)    | (£338)    |
| *Return on Capital*      | 15%       | 11%       |

|                          | *1979/80* | *1980/81* |
|--------------------------|-----------|-----------|
| **Pigs and Poultry**     |           |           |
| Average Size of Farm     | 138 Acres | 140 Acres |
|                          | £         | £         |
| Total Farm Output        | 110,192   | 122,740   |
| Total Farm Inputs        | 98,405    | 110,085   |
| Net Farm Income          | 11,787    | 12,655    |
| Average Tenant's Capital | 76,820    | 86,341    |
| (per acre)               | (£557)    | (£616)    |
| *Return on Capital*      | 15%       | 15%       |

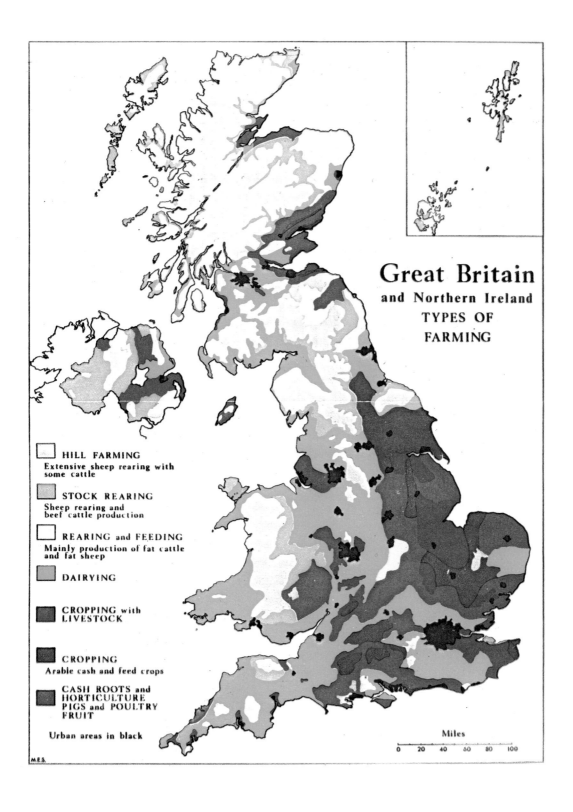

**Great Britain**
and Northern Ireland
TYPES OF
FARMING

HILL FARMING
Extensive sheep rearing with
some cattle

STOCK REARING
Sheep rearing and
beef cattle production

REARING and FEEDING
Mainly production of fat cattle
and fat sheep

DAIRYING

CROPPING with
LIVESTOCK

CROPPING
Arable cash and feed crops

CASH ROOTS and
HORTICULTURE
PIGS and POULTRY
FRUIT

Urban areas in black

Miles
0   20   40   60   80   100

M.E.S.

# SOIL CLASSIFICATION MAP OF GREAT BRITAIN

**Jones Lang Wootton**
Chartered Surveyors

103 Mount Street
London W1Y 6AS

01·493 6040

**Legend**

Normally high output cereals roots and vegetables with rotational grassland (English Grades 1 and 2).

Cereals or intensive grassland rotation (English Grade 3).

Predominantly livestock rearing, permanent pasture/rough grazing or forestry planting land (English Grades 4 and 5).

**N.B.**
This map is for general guidance only.

Scale 1:1,250,000

0  10  20  30  40  50  60  70  80  90  100 Miles

0  10  20  30  40  50        100              150 Kilometres

## GLUME BLOTCH (SEPTORIA NODORUM)

Unlike Eyespot, *Septoria* attacks leaves and ears of the crop. The symptoms show an attack of glume blotch with the production of pycnidia in the diseased tissue of the chaff.

## SOOTY MOULDS/
## COSMETIC EFFECTS OF FUNGICIDES

Sooty moulds often confused with the symptoms of *Septoria nodorum* are caused by secondary infections of *Cladosporium* moulds, and are symptomatic of primary attacks by parasitic fungi, aphid attack or adverse growing conditions. They will be controlled by a Bavistin spray at ear emergence; however, it is more important to identify the casual agent of the primary infection.

## HERBICIDE SCORCH

The lesions on this plant were caused by herbicide scorch and bear some similarity to those caused by *Rhynchosporium*. Pale green watery lesions are how-ever absent (see early *Rhynchosporium*)

Under stress conditions some varieties may show similar symptoms. Maris Mink and Mazurka are affected quite frequently.

## MANGANESE DEFICIENCY

Manganese and magnesium deficiencies are also some-times confused with *Rhynchosporium*.

## BARLEY YELLOW RUST

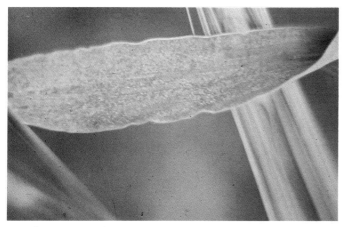

Symptoms of this disease are often not so clearly defined as in wheat. Development can be very rapid with postules breaking out over large areas of the leaf, obscuring the typical striped effect and causing rapid death of the leaves.

## WHEAT YELLOW RUST

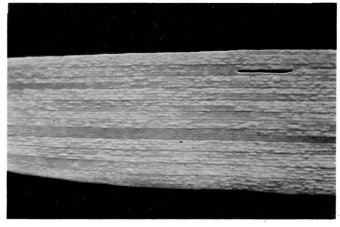

Yellow rust may not produce spores in such well defined lines early in the season as can be seen in this illustration.

## WHEAT BROWN & YELLOW RUST

Brown and yellow rust normally develop under different weather conditions. However, the variability of summer conditions in Great Britain can lead to development of both diseases as can be seen in the illustration.

## WHEAT EYESPOT

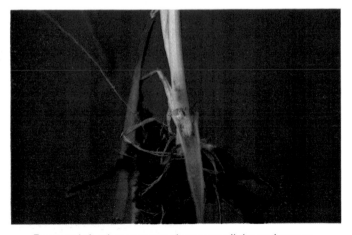

Eyespot infection can vary between slight and severe as shown on the four tillers above. Spraying should be carried out if 25% of the plants are infected in the spring.

## BARLEY MILDEW

Development of mildew in the spring barley crop can
be very rapid under favourable conditions. It is important not to let the disease damage the crop before
spraying. The symptoms shown above show the ideal
time to spray mildew if a preventative spray has not
been applied.

## BARLEY MILDEW

Later in the season black spore cases (perithecia) can
be seen in the white masses of mildew mycelia. These
black spore cases are resistant to weathering and
enable the disease to survive from harvest until the
winter crop or volunteers germinate.

# RHYNCHOSPORIUM (LEAF BLOTCH)

Some of the new potentially very high yielding and high quality barley varieties are very susceptible to this disease. The winter barley Maris Otter is also susceptible. Attacks of the disease cause progressive death of leaf tissue resulting in loss of yield and quality.

# BARLEY RHYNCHOSPORIUM

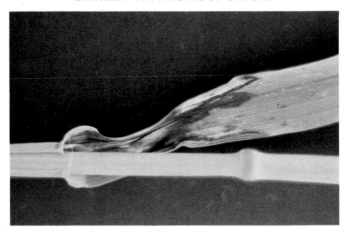

Under cool wet conditions *Rhynchosporium* may develop rapidly from primary infections in the crop. For accurate diagnosis of the disease it is essential to identify the typical pale green watery lesions in the early stages of disease developments as shown above.

CHAPTER 6

# Co-operatives in Agriculture

Co-operatives are a subject in themselves – this is why I have treated them separately, although in a sense they belong to the previous chapter on 'sources of finance'. Co-operatives may be thought of as a means of 'project finance'. There is no statutory definition but a co-operative may be briefly defined as: operating jointly to the same end, a union of persons for the production or distribution of goods for their common benefit.

There are currently over 500 co-operatives in the United Kingdom and the farming industry today is becoming more interested in co-operation encouraged by the Central Council for Agricultural and Horticultural Co-operation (CCAHC). This is therefore a subject well worth understanding as each request for finance will involve considerable funding – usually £1m. plus – and invariably each request will have to be treated on its own merit as the variation between co-operatives is marked.

## TYPES OF CO-OPERATIVE

There are three main types of co-operatives: marketing co-operatives, requisite co-operatives and service co-operatives. The marketing co-operative deals primarily with the marketing of farmer members' products *(outputs)*. Sometimes linked to a central crop store but not necessarily – e.g. a marketing co-operative could deal with selling pigs produced by a group of farmer members. The pigs could be supplied direct to the buyer and never brought to a central store.

The requisite co-operative deals with the supply of goods to farmer members – e.g. fertilizers, sprays and other farming *inputs*.

The service co-operative is concerned with the support of business *services* – e.g. farm secretarial work, agronomists etc.

Most requests for finance today come from newly formed marketing co-operatives where a central crop store is to be built so that the co-operative will be able to market farmer members' produce in bulk.

### Registration

Co-operatives may be registered either (a) under the Industrial and Provident

Societies Act 1965, or (b) as companies under the Companies Acts. The decision on whether a co-operative should be formed as a society or a company really lies with the farmer members, but advice can be obtained from CCAHC staff.

Whether a society or company, the share capital is normally kept to a minimum and does not feature as a significant source of funds. It is normal for farmer members to provide interest free loans as a method of member investment. The co-operative is for the benefit of its members and is not meant to be a profit-making concern, although in some circumstances interest on shares is paid. It is not necessary to accumulate excesses of reserves but the co-operative must, of course, have financial strength.

## Commitment

Commitment by the members to use the co-operative is essential. Usually for the project to be viable financially it is vital from the beginning to have an assured minimum volume for an agreed period of time. Commitment is usually dealt with in a form of members' agreement which is legally binding and each member will sign the agreement. To take a typical example – if the co-operative is setting up a 10,000 tonne* grain store and only has 8,000 tonnes stored when in use then the servicing cost per tonne may be too high. 10,000 tonnes is required, and once committed the farmer members should remain so, at least until any outside borrowing (for example the bank) has been repaid.

## Mutual status

Mutual status can be accepted by the Inspector of Taxes. To achieve this the co-operative must adhere to sound co-operative principles. These are briefly that:

(a) the business of the co-operative will be conducted for the mutual benefit of its members in such a way that the benefits obtained will stem from their participation in the business;

and

(b) any profits earned that are to be distributed will be distributed in relation to the extent to which the members have traded with, or taken part in, the business.

The acceptance of mutual status will mean that the co-operative is not liable to corporation tax on any operating surplus retained in the co-operative, provided that it is not excessive. This is, of course, a most useful consideration which enables co-operatives to make forward financial plans without undue tax consideration.

The disadvantage is that capital allowances are lost. But since such allowances are generally only a means of deferring tax payment, mutual status almost permanently eliminates any significant tax liabilities.

*Author's Note – metric measurement is usually used in co-operation projects. 1 tonne = 0.98 ton.

## FINANCING OF A MARKETING CO-OPERATIVE

The method commonly adopted is to obtain finance from farmer members; from grants and from bank borrowing. An approach which would be acceptable to the CCAHC when considering grant applications has the following broad structure:

| | | |
|---|---|---|
| Member investment | 33% | |
| Grant (UK only)* | 27% | the relative proportions will depend |
| Bank borrowing | 40% | upon rate of grant |
| Total | 100% | |

### Member Investment

Member investment is normally required to be approximately one third of the total capital cost – this is a Central Council requirement. Share capital does not need to provide a significant amount. Members' voting powers are not related to the amount of share-holding – it is normal for one farmer member to have one vote (votes are distributed equally among members and not in proportion to investment).

A form of interest free loan has become the most preferred and commonly accepted method of member investment, and is usually referred to as a *Qualification Loan.*

The details covering this loan will be included in the farmer member's agreement. The amount required from each farmer member will be directly related to his commitment to the co-operative – e.g. total capital cost for 11,000 tonne capacity grain store £1m. One third proportion to be invested by members – approximately £330,000. *Qualification Loan* therefore required for each tonne committed to store (£330,000 divided by 11,000) = £30. The qualification loan is regarded as a semi-permanent investment and the minimum period is covered by the initial term of the member's agreement which must cover time required to pay any outside borrowing – e.g. bank loan.

### Grants

There are UK grant schemes for which co-operatives can apply through the Central Council and also FEOGA grants† for which applications are made to Brussels through the appropriate agricultural department. The UK grant will be known promptly and it will therefore be acceptable to assume UK grant received in the financial projections. However, the same does not apply to the FEOGA grant and because of delay and uncertainty, the Central Council usually requires any financial project to show viability without taking into account any FEOGA grant. Should the FEOGA grant be received subsequently, this will of course be an additional benefit.

---

*Authors Note – due to uncertainty over receipt of any EEC grant, only the UK grant is usually taken into the initial projections.

†Author's Note – French name for section of European Agricultural Guarantee and Guidance Fund – for more detail see Chapter 8 on EEC.

Financial budgets have to be presented in support of the application and of course these will subsequently be necessary for production to the bank. In our example, in order to obtain a grant the *initial* member commitment would have to be at least 80% of the total capacity of the store. This 80% commitment is a special concession by the Central Council to ease the problem of 100% capacity not being covered by members' commitment at the time the building works have to start. It will be expected, however, that *full commitment* must be achieved within a *specified time*.

### Bank Borrowing

The banker will ascertain at the outset whether he is dealing with a co-operative registered under the Industrial Provident Societies Act or the Companies Act. In either case the bank should see the set of rules or the Memorandum and Articles of Association. The bank will usually require, with this large type of project finance, financial forecasts and cash flows and a detailed report of feasibility. The bank will be particularly interested in the security available and the evidence of the ability of the co-operative to service and repay any loan request.

It is usual during the building period for a bridging facility to be required owing to the delay in receiving UK grant monies. Funding can be on overdraft or loan but it is usual to structure this on a loan repayable over a fixed period. A bank might require the following:

1. estimates for building and capital expenditure;
2. a specified degree of commitment by farmer members – the minimum might be 80% as required by Central Council;
3. the farmer members' agreement containing suitable safeguards that throughput is assured;
4. a satisfactory amount of member investment to be actually received and used on the project before the co-operative starts using the bank facility;
5. grant monies received to be notified to the bank and not used to repay member investment without first negotiating with the bank;
6. UK grant approval to be confirmed before any bank facility will be implemented.

### Security

This would normally be a first charge by way of debenture in favour of the bank on all the assets of the co-operative, including the members' agreements. Sometimes guarantees may be available from farmer members. The co-operative should also consider the loan guarantee scheme operated in conjunction with the Agricultural Credit Corporation (see Chapter 5) – but there is a limit to the amount that they will cover in dealing with co-operatives. (Details will be given by Central Council.)

### Professional Advice

The financial considerations in forming a new co-operative are complex and Central Council staff are available to help and advise in the member deliberations.*

*The address of CCAHC is: Market Towers, New Covent Garden Market, London, SW8 5NQ. The Council also has 10 regional offices.

## Depreciation in a Marketing Co-operative

When an asset is purchased, the transaction is treated in the accounts as a capital cost – not as a revenue cost. When the purchase is made in part or wholly with the bank loan the repayment of that loan is not a revenue cost.

The principle behind depreciation in the accounts is to charge as a revenue expense a proportion of the cost each year which will write off the asset over its effective working life. This is a real cost which cannot be ignored by the co-operative. The cost of depreciation should be included in the service charge paid by the members. Thus depreciation will bring in an annual inflow of cash and will be a source of funds towards the annual bank loan repayments in the early years.

## Grant Aid in Co-operative Accounts

There are two methods of showing this:

| | | |
|---|---|---|
| 1. | Gross cost of asset | £10,000 |
| | *Less* grant (25%) | 2,500 |
| | Net cost in balance sheet | 7,500 |
| | Annual depreciation – cash inflow | 750 |
| 2. | Gross cost of asset (in balance sheet) | £10,000 |
| | Grant reserve (in balance sheet) | 2,500 |
| | Annual depreciation | 1,000 |
| | Annual grant – write back | 250 |
| | Net cash inflow | 750 |

The second method is usually recommended by Central Council. It is considered preferable because of its more informative presentation. Also of course, with the first method, the balance sheet is weakened by under-stating the value of the assets.

## Budgets, Operating Costs and Service Charges to Members

CCAHC has published a very useful booklet – 'A Director's Guide to Financing Marketing Co-operatives' (1981) by W. L. G. Absalom, FCMA – in which it is suggested that one useful management technique is to adopt a suitable system of budgetary control and forecasting appropriate to the size and operation of the co-operative: it is important to take a view about the future of the co-operative and its objectives (a plan), to express this in financial terms (a budget), and to compare actual results with budget to establish those areas which need attention (action).

Taking an imaginary society, CCAHC have produced simple examples of budgets which it would be advisable to prepare in advance of a major building project. An extract from the CCAHC booklet is reproduced on pages 91–98.

**Leasing in Co-operatives**

Generally speaking, as most marketing co-operatives need to invest heavily in grant aided assets, leasing tends to be unattractive as grants will not be paid on assets which are leased.

## SUMMARY ON CO-OPERATIVE FINANCING

As mentioned at the start, this type of project finance is complex. In our example the bank would need to ensure:

1. that the project has the capability of pay-back of loan finance;
2. that it is satisfied with the proposed management structure and farmer member commitment. This is a particularly important point as without commitment from the farmer members the project will not succeed;
3. that the farmer members are reasonably well spread geographically to reduce the possible risk of harvest or other farming failure;
4. that security – normally debenture and the bank's debenture cover – is monitored carefully. (Also it will be necessary to bear in mind that the building is most likely to be highly specialised and the value in the event of a forced sale could be questionable.)

## CO-OPERATIVE SOCIETY BUDGETS

(Extract from 'A Director's Guide to Financing Marketing Co-operatives' (1981)

The following sets out simple examples of budgets which it is advisable to prepare in advance of a major project. We will assume that a new storage and marketing co-operative is being formed, which will acquire a building and machinery. Land is estimated to cost £5,000, and buildings and machinery £750,500, on which grant-aid will average 28.0 per cent. The capacity will be 11,000 tonnes, with commitment, achieved in year 1, of 10,000 tonnes; year 2, 10,500 tonnes; and year 3, 11,000 tonnes. The financial year-end will be 31 July. Building will commence in December 1981 and be completed in September 1982; that is, after the end of the run-up year on 31 July 1982. The first year of operation will end on 31 July 1983. Increases for inflation have not been included, in order not to cloud the effects of volume and the reducing bank interest costs.

Six schedules have been prepared, as follows:

Figure 1    Broad financial plan
Figure 2    Depreciation and grant calculations
Figure 3    Initial monthly cash flow for bridging loan
Figure 4    Budgeted operating costs
Figure 5    Forecast annual cash flow
Figure 6    Forecast balance sheets

Explanatory notes are given for each, and there is an inter-relationship. These schedules will form the basis for a grant application, for negotiations with the banks, and for directing the financial affairs of the co-operative.

**The Molasba Society Ltd**                                    **Figure 1**

### Broad Financial Plan

|  |  | £ |
|---|---|---|
| *Costs* | | |
| | Land – Freehold | 5,000 |
| | Buildings and Machinery | 750,000 |
| | Run-up Year (Figure 4) | 28,335 |
| | | 783,335 |
| *Financing* | | |
| | Members' Qualification Loans | |
| | (11,000 tonnes @ £22.5 per tonne) | 247,500 |
| | UK Grant (Figure 2) | 210,000 |
| | Balance Bank Loan | 325,835 |
| | | 783,335 |

### Notes to Figure 1

1. The cost of the run-up year has been included in this schedule, because it has to be financed. As explained later, part of it could be treated as an additional capital cost. In this exercise it has been treated as a revenue cost.

2. Qualification loans should approximate one-third of the capital cost of the project to meet the normal requirements of Central Council when a grant application is being made. The amount is then divided by the total practical capacity, to arrive at the amount required per tonne of commitment.

3. At this stage the indications are that, after the bridging loan period, a bank loan of £325,835 will be required.

   From Figure 2 the cash flow from depreciation, net of grant write-back, is estimated at £40,790. This indicates that the loan repayment period required is 8 years, subject to the final actual figures, once these become known.

   We will assume that a bank loan of £326,000 is negotiated, to be repaid over 8 years, with equal annual repayment of principal of £40,750.

### The Molasba Society Ltd                                          Figure 2

#### Depreciation and Grant Calculations

| Life of Asset Group | 40 Years £ | 15 Years £ | 10 Years £ | 5 Years £ | Total £ |
|---|---|---|---|---|---|
| Capital Cost | 300,000 | 131,000 | 249,000 | 70,000 | 750,000 |
| Annual Historical Depreciation (Capital Cost divided by years) | 7,500 | 8,735 | 24,900 | 14,000 | 55,135 |
| UK Grant: Rate | $32\frac{1}{2}$% | 25% | 25% | 25% | 28% |
| Amount | 97,500 | 32,750 | 62,250 | 17,500 | 210,000 |
| Annual Grant Write-back (Grant divided by years) | 2,440 | 2,180 | 6,225 | 3,500 | 14,345 |
| Net Annual Cash Flow (Depreciation less Grant Write-back) | | | | | 40,790 |

### Notes to Figure 2

1. As already explained, a realistic anticipated life of each asset should be used.

2. Land has not been included above, since it has been earlier defined as freehold which is not depreciated.

3. If some of the run-up costs are to be capitalised, then that amount must be included in the above for depreciation purposes.

4. In the above grant calculations, the percentage rate has been applied to the total capital cost of each asset group. In practice there may be certain items on which grant is not paid and this should be checked.

**Figure 3**

# The Molasba Society Ltd

## Initial Monthly Cash Flow for Bridging Loan to 31 July 1983

| Month | INFLOW | | | | | OUTFLOW | | | |
|---|---|---|---|---|---|---|---|---|---|
| | Qualification Loans £ | UK Grant £ | Service Charges £ | Capital Costs £ | Run-up Costs £ | Operating Costs £ | Monthly Surplus (Deficit) £ | Monthly Bank Interest £ | Bank Balance (Overdraft) £ |
| *1981* | | | | | | | | | |
| November | 30* | | | 5,000 | | | (4,970) | 63 | (4,970) |
| December | 112,500 | | | 90,000 | | | 22,500 | 175Cr | 17,530 |
| *1982* | | | | | | | | | |
| January | 67,500 | | | 150,000 | | | (82,500) | 812 | (65,670) |
| February | 45,000 | | | 100,000 | | | (55,000) | 1,510 | (120,670) |
| March | | | | 100,000 | 500 | | (100,000) | 2,765 | (221,170) |
| April | | 100,000 | | 70,000 | 500 | | 29,500 | 2,395 | (191,670) |
| May | | | | 90,000 | 1,600 | | (91,600) | 3,540 | (283,270) |
| June | | 50,000 | | 75,000 | 2,700 | | (27,700) | 3,890 | (310,970) |
| July | | | | 40,000 | 3,800 | | (43,800) | 4,435 | (373,305) |
| **Total** | 225,000 | 150,000 | — | 720,000 | 9,100 | — | | 19,235 | |
| August | | | | | | 10,000 | (10,000) | 4,790 | (383,305) |
| September | | 50,000 | 75,000 | | | 10,000 | 115,000 | 3,355 | (268,305) |
| October | | | 75,000 | | | 24,400 | 50,600 | 2,720 | (217,705) |
| November | 10* | | | | | 4,500 | (4,490) | 2,780 | (222,195) |
| December | | | | 35,000 | | 1,500 | (36,500) | 3,235 | (258,695) |
| *1983* | | | | | | | | | |
| January | | 10,000 | | | | 2,000 | 8,000 | 3,135 | (270,710) |
| February | 6,750 | | | | | 1,500 | 5,250 | 3,320 | (265,460) |
| March | 4,500 | | | | | 1,400 | 3,100 | 3,280 | (262,360) |
| April | | | | | | 1,400 | (1,400) | 3,300 | (263,760) |
| May | | | | | | 1,300 | (1,300) | 3,310 | (265,060) |
| June | | | | | | 1,700 | (1,700) | 3,335 | (266,760) |
| July | | | | | | 1,500 | (1,500) | 3,355 | (288,160) |
| **Total** | 11,250 | 60,000 | 150,000 | 35,000 | — | 61,200 | | 39,915 | |
| Outstanding | 11,250 | | | | | | | | |
| Grand Totals (Fig. 1) | 247,500 | 210,000 | | 755,000 | | | | | |

\* Shares excluded from totals.

## Notes to Figure 3

1. *Approximations*
   Certain figures in this schedule have been roughly estimated and serve only to illustrate the techniques. Even in practice an initial high degree of accuracy is unlikely, but this must not discourage a good attempt.

2. *Qualification Loans*
   Remember that commitment for the first year was only 10,000 tonnes, followed by 500 tonnes in each of the next 2 years. Qualification loans for the latter have been estimated to be received in February and March of each year.
   Delay in achieving full commitment for the facilities means higher bank borrowing and thereby higher bank interest. Rather than the initial members bearing the brunt, the cost is averaged over the first few years, so that the late joiners pay their fair share (see Figure 4).

3. *Capital Payments and UK Grants*
   Claiming for UK grant follows payment for identifiable stages of completion. To minimise bank interest costs, the claims should be presented promptly.
   Since initial commitment is greater than 80 per cent of the whole, payment of grant has been anticipated (see Chapter 2 (ii)).

4. *Service Charges*
   In order to relieve the cash flow of the co-operative, it is often decided to require members to pay their full service charges early in the season. We have assumed 50 per cent in September and 50 per cent in October. At the time of preparing Schedule 3, the income has to be estimated because the service charge has not yet been calculated. In this illustration, the income was estimated at £150,000 whereas in the event it was £144,000 (see Figure 4). This difference is too small to require any recalculations.

5. *Run-up Costs*
   This cost is shown in Figure 4. The bank interest has to be added. Sometimes part of this cost is capitalised as a legitimate cost of the project, but this has not been introduced in this example. Instead it is planned to recoup the run-up cost in the service charge averaged over the first 3 years of actual operation (see Figure 4).

6. *Bank Interest*
   The percentage rate has to be estimated. It has been assumed in this example that the interest is added to the overdraft at the end of July and January. It has, of course, been calculated monthly in the period shown. For subsequent years a reasonable annual estimate is made, remembering the annual reduction of principal.

7. *Operating Costs*
   As earlier explained, depreciation does not incur a cash outflow. Note also on this schedule that bank interest is shown separately. Hence the outflow shown under operating costs does not include these two items. The total is obtained from Figure 4, and the month of expenditure estimated; for example, it is likely that the haulage costs will have to be paid early in the season.
   All costs are recovered in the service charge to members.

8. *Bank Overdraft*
   This schedule covers the period when a bridging loan is required. In this example the peak is reached in August 1982 and the bank facility should be fixed with a little to spare.

## The Molasba Society Ltd                                    Figure 4

### Budgeted Operating Costs

| Year ending 31 July | 1981/82 | 1982/83 | 1983/84 | 1984/85 |
|---|---|---|---|---|
| Tonnes Throughput | Run-up | 10,000 | 10,500 | 11,000 |
| Operating Expenses | £ | £ | £ | £ |
| Payroll Costs: | | | | |
| Management | 4,000 | 8,000 | 8,500 | 9,000 |
| Office | — | 2,000 | 2,000 | 2,000 |
| Works staff | — | 4,000 | 4,000 | 4,000 |
| Casual Labour | — | 3,000 | 3,200 | 3,300 |
| Haulage In (£2.50 per tonne) | — | 25,000 | 26,250 | 27,500 |
| Fuel oil | 2,000 | 10,000 | 10,500 | 11,000 |
| Electricity | 300 | 2,000 | 2,100 | 2,200 |
| Chemicals | — | 200 | 200 | 200 |
| Maintenance & Repairs | — | 2,000 | 3,000 | 6,000 |
| Insurance | — | 3,000 | 3,200 | 3,300 |
| Telephone & Postage | 250 | 600 | 700 | 700 |
| Stationery & Printing | 50 | 400 | 400 | 400 |
| General Expenses | 500 | 500 | 500 | 600 |
| Professional & Audit | 2,000 | 500 | 500 | 500 |
| Depreciation (Figure 2) | — | 55,135 | 55,135 | 55,135 |
| Bank Interest (Figure 3) | 19,235 | 39,915 | 34,000 | 28,000 |
| | 28,335 | 156,250 | 154,185 | 153,835 |
| Less grant write-back (Figure 2) | — | 14,345 | 14,345 | 14,345 |
| Net operating expenses | 28,335 | 141,905 | 139,840 | 139,490 |
| Actual service cost per tonne | — | 14.19 | 13.32 | 12.68 |

| Income | | | | |
|---|---|---|---|---|
| Calculated service charge | | | | |
| @ £14.40 per tonne | — | 144,000 | 151,200 | 158,400 |
| Surplus (Deficiency) | (28,335) | 2,095 | 11,360 | 18,910 |
| Cumulative Surplus (Deficiency) | (28,335) | (26,240) | (14,880) | 4,030 |

## Notes to Figure 4

1. *Service Cost Per Tonne*

   This demonstrates how the cost per tonne reduces with the increased volume and the decreasing bank interest. Remember that the effects of inflation have not been included. Because of the cumulative loss, due to the run-up period, the actual costs per tonne cannot yet be used. Instead the average cost per tonne has been calculated by taking the total net costs for the 4 years, dividing by the aggregate of the tonnage throughput, and rounding upwards in order to produce a small cumulative surplus at the end of the period.

   This service charge has to be acceptable to potential members considering joining the project. An aspect to explain to them is that once the cumulative deficit has been eliminated, the annual service cost per tonne might be reduced – always bearing in mind the resulting cash flow and the need to conserve some in readiness to replace assets (some may need replacing after 5 years).

   With understanding and a little practice, the operation of this simple form of budgetary control allows directors to ensure that the interests of members and of their co-operative can be harmonised for the common good.

2. *Need to Avoid Losses*

   It will be appreciated that if losses are made continually, the cash flow will be adversely affected and bank loan repayments may suffer. This must be avoided.

   Two causes of loss are:

   a) Insufficient volume – hence the importance of commitment by members in terms of both quantity and time.

   b) Optimistic estimates of likely service charges when first trying to attract potential members, followed by a reluctance to charge realistically.

3. *Mutuality*

   Although somewhat academic at this early stage, tax liability has not been considered, on the assumption that mutual status will be granted by the Inspector of Taxes.

4. *Items of Cost*

   The items shown are only representative. Since it has been assumed that mutual status will be achieved, no interest on members' investment has been included.

   Rates have also been excluded, but currently (1981) this needs careful consideration.

## The Molasba Society Ltd

**Figure 5**

### Forecast Annual Cash Flow to 31 July 1985

| Year ending 31 July | 1982 £ | 1983 £ | 1984 £ | 1985 £ |
|---|---|---|---|---|
| *Outflow* | | | | |
| Capital Expenditure (Figure 3) | 720,000 | 35,000 | — | — |
| Operating Loss (Figure 4) | 28,335 | — | — | — |
| Bank Loan repayment (Figure 1) | — | 40,750 | 40,750 | 40,750 |
| | 748,335 | 75,750 | 40,750 | 40,750 |
| | | | | |
| *Inflow* | | | | |
| Operating Profit (Figure 4) | — | 2,095 | 11,360 | 18,910 |
| Depreciation (Figure 2) | — | 55,135 | 55,135 | 55,135 |
| Grant Write-back (Figure 2) | — | (14,345) | (14,345) | (14,345) |
| Qualification Loans (Figure 3) | 225,000 | 11,250 | 11,250 | — |
| UK Grant (Figure 3) | 150,000 | 60,000 | — | — |
| Shares (Figure 3) | 30 | 10 | 10 | — |
| | 375,030 | 114,145 | 63,410 | 59,700 |
| | | | | |
| Net In (Out) | (373,305) | 38,395 | 22,660 | 18,950 |
| Bank Loan opening | — | — | (285,250) | (244,500) |
| closing | — | (285,250) | (244,500) | (203,750) |
| | | | | |
| Overdraft opening | — | (373,305) | (8,910) | 13,750 |
| closing | (373,305) | (8,910) | 13,750 | 32,700 |

### Note to Figure 5

1. Despite the bank loan, there is also a credit balance in the current account by July 1984. In practice, the two balances may be combined to reduce bank interest. Remember, however, that since cash will be required to replace certain assets after 5 years (Figure 2), the bank loan facility will require regular review.

## The Molasba Society Ltd                                    Figure 6

### Forecast Balance Sheets – Year ending 31 July

|  | 1982 £ | 1983 £ | 1984 £ | 1985 £ |
|---|---|---|---|---|
| Fixed Assets at cost | 720,000 | 755,000 | 755,000 | 755,000 |
| Less cumulative depreciation | — | 55,135 | 110,270 | 165,405 |
|  | 720,000 | 699,865 | 644,730 | 589,595 |
| Net Current Assets | — | — | — | — |
| Bank Balance (Overdraft) | (373,305) | (8,910) | 13,750 | 32,700 |
|  | 346,695 | 690,955 | 658,480 | 622,295 |
| Financed by: |  |  |  |  |
| Shares | 30 | 40 | 50 | 50 |
| Qualification Loans | 225,000 | 236,250 | 247,500 | 247,500 |
| Grant Reserve | 150,000 | 195,655 | 181,310 | 166,965 |
| Bank Loan | — | 285,250 | 244,500 | 203,750 |
| Retained Surplus (Deficiency) | (28,335) | (26,240) | (14,880) | 4,030 |
|  | 346,695 | 690,955 | 658,480 | 622,295 |

### Notes to Figure 6

1. At the end of July 1982, the bank bridging facility is still in operation. However, at the end of July 1983 we have introduced the bank loan, which was negotiated (Figure 1) as £326,000, with an annual repayment of £40,750.

2. Note the healthy appearance, with the gross cost of assets and a grant reserve being shown. The latter is being reduced by the grant write-back, which reduces the operating costs in Figure 4.

3. In practice there may well be certain current assets (stock, debtors etc) and current liabilities (creditors etc) but, for ease of presentation, these have been assumed to balance out.

*     *     *     *

The six schedules illustrated in this section are examples of budgetary control as a technique towards overall financial control. The assumption has been made that the co-operative deals only with a single type of produce. Should its operations involve completely different products with different facilities, it becomes most important to have separate operating accounts for each major section.

CHAPTER 7

# Taxation

I am not a tax expert and would not pretend to be. There are many aspects to be considered. In addition to the farmer's own accountant and other professional advisers, most of the banks have specialist taxation departments which are used to dealing with farming and other business tax problems. However, there are some general points worth stating *in outline only*.

### Income Tax

Most farm businesses are run by a sole farmer or on a partnership basis. Farmers are treated as 'carrying on a trade' and assessed for income tax under Schedule D, Case 1.

### Profit Averaging

This is a basis on which farm businesses other than companies may claim to average profits over two consecutive years (but is not available for opening and closing years). The profits in the lower year must be no more than 70% of the profits of the higher year. Limited spreading is allowed if the lower profits are marginally higher than the 70% figure.

In making the profit calculation it is necessary to calculate profit before deduction of capital allowances or stock relief. Although, of course, those reliefs will be available to be given from the averaged profits figure.

### Stock Relief

Tax relief has been given in recent years to allow for increases in trading stock values resulting from inflation. The system is being changed in 1982/83 in that relief will be calculated by reference to an all-stock index which will then be applied to the stock value calculation.

### Herd Basis

You will frequently come across this. Farmers can elect for 'production' herds (e.g. a dairy herd or ewe flock) to be treated on a 'herd basis' for taxation rather than the usual trading stock basis. This means that valuations are *not* taken into account in arriving at the annual profit and loss. Also on disposal (or substantial disposal) of the herd the farmer pays no tax on any profit over the original cost price. (Nor is there any relief for loss.)

## Capital Expenditure Allowances

### Machinery and Plant
Allowances are given on both new and second-hand machinery. A first year allowance of 100% is available but need not be taken in full. Any balance can be added to a 'pool' figure.

Motorcars are separated from the 'pool' for taxation and a writing down allowance of 25% is available on the adjusted pool figure. The balance is then carried forward to the next year.

### Buildings
If expenditure is incurred on construction, reconstruction, extension, alteration or improvement of farmhouses, buildings, cottages, fences and other works, an allowance can be claimed up to 30% in the first year and then 10% annually in the next seven years.

## Capital Gains Tax

This is a tax payable on gains arising from the disposal of chargeable assets by way of sale, gift, lease etc. The gain is the difference between the purchase price plus costs and the sale price less costs and is taxed at a rate of 30%.

For certain assets acquired before April 1965 an election can be made to take the value as at 6 April 1965 in order to restrict the gain to the net sale proceeds *less* the 1965 valuation. This is particularly important for assets such as farmland in view of the substantial rise in land prices over the years.

No capital gains tax charge arises on death nor on gifts between husband and wife. Certain tax exemptions are made available at the time of retirement and related to the individual's retirement age.

'Roll-over relief' allows payment of capital gains tax due on the disposal of qualifying business assets to be deferred, provided the disposal proceeds are reinvested in qualifying assets. Qualifying assets are, basically, farming assets.

## Capital Transfer Tax

Capital transfer tax is chargeable on property which changes hands by way of gift during lifetime and on death. At the time of writing, the main exemptions are:

i Gifts and bequests from husband to wife and vice versa.
ii Transfers not exceeding £3,000 per annum. (Any balance unused may be carried forward to the following year only.)
iii Gifts to any number of persons not exceeding £250 each, per annum
iv Gifts made out of income provided *sufficient* income remains to maintain the donor's standard of living.

  v Wedding gifts – £5,000 limit for a parent of either party to the marriage; £2,500 if a grand-parent or great grand-parent; £1,000 for any other person.

  vi Certain gifts to charities and political parties.

After deduction of exemptions, the first £55,000 of chargeable transfers is not taxed. Above that figure, further chargeable transfers attract tax at increasing rates.

*Agricultural relief* – the value of agricultural property is reduced by 50% to qualifying farmers. (A farmer must have derived more than 75% of his earnings from farming in any five of the last seven years in order to qualify.)

The relief is limited to £250,000 or 1000 acres whichever is the most favourable.

*Business relief* is available on 'business assets' transferred (including tenant's assets). If the 50% agricultural relief is not available, e.g. where the farmer does not 'qualify', then this relief may be available – the value of the business assets being reduced by 50% for CTT purposes.

Payment of tax can be made in certain cases by either eight yearly or 16 half-yearly instalments.

*Planning*

    to meet CTT liabilities is something to be seriously considered by the farmer as land values can generate a high value estate, e.g. a 500 acre farm valued at say £2,000 per acre means an estate value of £1m. Even after deduction of the 50% agricultural relief, CTT of *£237,500* could be payable at current rates.

*Consider*

    *Lifetime transfer gifts* attract a lower rate of tax – in the example above £132,500 would be payable and the beneficiary could elect to pay tax over eight years.*

    *Provision of a fund* to meet tax liabilities – usually by way of life insurance policy. This must be drawn up correctly to ensure that the policy proceeds do not attract a tax liability on the death of the insured.

    *Draw up a will* and consider equalisation of estates between farmer and wife. They can each then give away £55,000 tax free. This action will substantially reduce the total tax payable. (See example below.)

    Use of annual gift exemptions (£3,000 per annum) – will help to reduce the ultimate tax liability.

## CTT EXAMPLE

| | | |
|---|---|---|
| A 400 acre farm worth say | £700,000 | (including land and stock etc.) |
| *less* Agricultural Relief (50%) | 350,000 | |
| Taxable Estate | £350,000 | |

*Tax Payable by Survivor £147,500*

* Editor's note: several recent changes affecting lifetime gifts generally make the CTT burden less onerous

Same Farm but equalise estates:

| Husband | | Wife | |
|---|---|---|---|
| Farm worth | £350,000 | Farm worth | £350,000 |
| *less* relief | 175,000 | *less* relief | 175,000 |
| Taxable Estate | £175,000 | Taxable Estate | £175,000 |
| Tax payable | £47,500 | Tax payable | £47,500 |

*Total payable £95,000*

*Tax saving £52,500*

As mentioned at the beginning of this Chapter, taxation, especially CTT, is a highly complex area and professional advice is definitely called for, whether from the bank's own specialists or from a local accountant. The rules of the game are constantly changing!

For further reading, there is a useful handbook entitled *Tax on the Farm* published by the National Farmers' Union.

CHAPTER 8

# The European Economic Community

## TREATY OF ROME

The basic principles on which the Common Agricultural Policy (CAP) was to be built were set out and signed by the six original member states in 1957. These were:

   i  to increase agricultural productivity
  ii  to ensure a fair standard of living for those in farming
 iii  to stabilize markets
 iv  to ensure reasonable consumer prices.

### The Member States

The United Kingdom, Denmark and Ireland joined in *1973* to form the nine member states (the EEC9).

|  | *Population* |
|---|---|
| Belgium | 10m. |
| Denmark | 5m. |
| France | 53m. |
| Germany | 62m. |
| Ireland | 3m. |
| Italy | 56m. |
| Luxembourg | ⅓m. |
| Netherlands | 14m. |
| United Kingdom | 56m. |
| Total population | 260m. |

Greece joined the community in 1981, and Spain and Portugal have requested accession (see below page 110).

## Production Facts

The importance of agriculture in the EEC9 can readily be seen from the latest figures available:

| | 1976–78 Averages | Production of EEC9 | |
| --- | --- | --- | --- |
| *Product* | *World production in tons* | *Percentage of world production* | *EEC9's world ranking* |
| Cereals (inc. rice) | 1,514.8 | 6.9% | 5 |
| Potatoes | 266.9 | 13.2% | 3 |
| Vegetables | 319.0 | 8.9% | 3 |
| Fruits | 259.0 | 14.4% | 1 |
| Sugar | 89.4 | 12.8% | 1 |
| Olive oil | 1.4 | 30% | 1 |
| Cows milk | 401.7 | 24.1% | 1 |
| Butter | 6.8 | 26.4% | 1 |
| Cheese | 10.2 | 29.7% | 1 |
| Beef & veal | 46.6 | 13.8% | 3 |
| Pig meat | 47.6 | 18.6% | 2 |
| Poultry meat | 24.6 | 14.0% | 2 |
| Sheep meat & goat meat | 7.3 | 6.9% | 4 |

A number of first places!
(Plus *wine* at number one with 45% of World Production.)


# EUROPEAN COMMUNITY INSTITUTIONS

There are four main institutions involved in the running of the Community:

## 1. The Council of Ministers

function –      the Community's principal decision-making body.

composition –   the Government of each nation in the Community has a seat on the Council.


## 2. The Commission

functions –     proposes Community policy and is responsible for administration.

composition –   the commission has 13 members chosen by agreement of the Community governments. Commisioners are usually appointed for four years.

### 3. The European Parliament

functions –
    (i) advises the Council of Minsters
    (ii) with the Council of Ministers, determines the budget for the Community
    (iii) exercises some practical control over the Council and Commission.

composition – 410 elected members representing the citizens of the Community.

### 4. The Court of Justice

functions – settles legal disputes involving Community laws.
composition – nine judges, one from each Community country.

## COMMON AGRICULTURAL POLICY

The main methods used in operating the Policy are:

1. *The Common External Tariff* which protects farmers from imports from non-member countries.
2. *'Intervention'* buying when produce is withdrawn from the market in times of surplus. Payments are also made for storage and export subsidies.
3. *Grants*
    – to assist changes in farm size structure;
    – to improve marketing through the co-operatives;
    – for training and re-training programmes;
    – for farm improvements.

The basic mechanism is:

### E.E.C. PRICE LEVEL

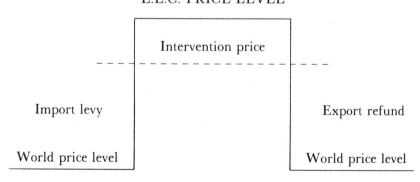

(a) The import levy raises world prices to EEC levels.
(b) The intervention price is the level at which the EEC authorities will buy and store commodities – a market of last resort – to keep the price up.

(c) The export refund is the reverse of the import levy. This repayment to exporters makes it possible to export from the high priced EEC market to low priced world markets.

## FINANCE

*Finance* to implement CAP objectives comes from:
1.  the European Agricultural Guarantee and Guidance Fund (EAGGF – usually known as FEOGA – French name);
2.  national governments.

### EAGGF
This is split into two sections:

The *Guidance* Section spends only a small proportion of the EEC budget in helping to finance projects for improving structure of production; processing and marketing; regional schemes and grants.

The *Guarantee* Section takes the 'lions share' and embraces almost all spending on market operations: guarantees prices; export refunds; intervention buying etc.

1981 EEC Budget*

| EAGGF | £m. | £m. |
|---|---|---|
| Guarantees section | 7,599 | |
| Guidance section | 318 | 7,917 (63%) |
| Other community activity | | 4,914 |
| | | 12,831 |

Within the Guarantee Section, price support for the Dairy Sector is the most expensive of the main items:

| | £m. |
|---|---|
| Dairy products | 2,552 |
| Cereals | 1,305 |
| Beef and veal | 1,197 |

With the EAGGF attracting 63% of the total Community budget – this has led to criticism particularly with spending at such a high level on the Dairy Sector which is currently in a surplus of production.

*Raising the Money*
This is a politically sensitive area. Readers may recall that in 1980, for example, it was estimated that the UK would be a net contributor to the extent of £1,100

*Data source, EEC Commission Report L/305

million. Following protracted discussions, the UK contribution was reduced in May 1980 but the basic methods of raising funds still are:

- customs duties
- levies on food imports
- a proportion of VAT (currently 1%)

These items accrue to the Community and *not* the member country.

Probably the most contentious problem is that member states producing more than they consume of price supported products are net recipients from the EEC budget. States that benefit include Denmark, Netherlands, and France.

Other member states not being surplus producers themselves are net contributors to the budget and these include the UK and Germany.

*Green Money*

CAP guaranteed prices are stated in European Currency Units (ECUs) which is a 'basket' unit whose value is based on weighted averages of the values of the EEC currencies. The farm prices are then converted into national currencies but this has been complicated by two different rates of exchange evolving:

  i The real value of the pound in ECUs as stated within the world's money markets. Hence variations occur daily.
 ii The 'green' value of the pound in ECUs is decided politically by our own government but has also to be agreed by the Council of Ministers. This rate changes only at long intervals and therefore avoids the difficult situation which would occur if farm prices had to be calculated daily.

The current *green rate* is         £1=1.61641 ECUs
                          or  1 E.C.U.=£0.62 approx.
The *actual spot value* is         £1=1.78603 ECUs
                        (as at March 1982)

The gap is therfore 9% and this reflects the strong pound in that the market rate is above the 'green rate'. This is unusual as for most of the period since the UK joined the EEC the 'green rate' was above the market rate to protect the U.K. consumer from higher food and farm prices. The following chart (see p. 108) illustrates how the gap changed from negative to positive during 1980.

The introduction of 'green rates' was not, of course, confined to the UK. Other member states also wished to protect either producers or consumers and introduced their own 'green rates'.

Hence movement of commodities would be affected between countries if there were no adjustment at frontiers. For example exports from a country with a *depreciated* currency would be *cheaper* and may well disturb the economy of a country where the currency had remained stable or had been revalued.

To limit deflections of trade the Community introduced a system of *Monetary Compensatory Amounts*, the level of which depends on the difference between the market exchange rate and the green rate. As the name suggests the MCA's

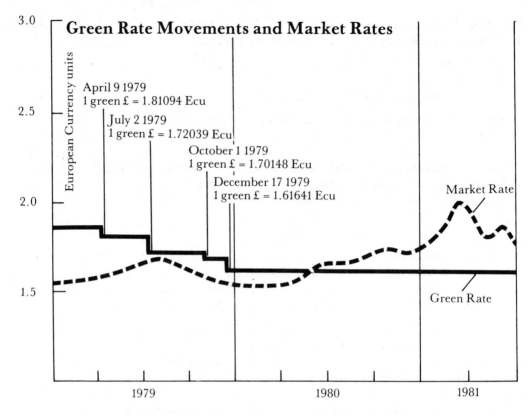

**Green Rate Movements and Market Rates**

European Currency units

April 9 1979
1 green £ = 1.81094 Ecu

July 2 1979
1 green £ = 1.72039 Ecu

October 1 1979
1 green £ = 1.70148 Ecu

December 17 1979
1 green £ = 1.61641 Ecu

Market Rate

Green Rate

1979      1980      1981

compensate for monetary change. They subsidise imports into countries with depreciated currencies and levy a charge on imports into countries with appreciating currencies.

The positive UK 'gap' at the moment of 9% between the green rate and market rate means that our exports attract subsidies and our CAP imports attract levies, thus generating positive MCAs to the UK at present. This turnaround is part of the reason why there has been more emphasis recently on farmers exporting.

The following is an example of how an export subsidy could apply:

UK exporter of calves to France for veal. Price per calf = 100 ECUs
1 ECU = £0.62 (green rate)
but market rate moves as sterling strengthens to 1 ECU £0.55 (market rate).

Therefore funds received per calf

|          |       |
|----------|-------|
| falls from | £62 |
| to       | £55   |
|          | −£7   |

Exporter therefore receives a positive MCA payment of £7 per calf. (Less 1% levy to EEC funds.)

## THE PRICE SUPPORT SYSTEM

Support systems for different commodities differ in detail, but basically all major products except potatoes are covered by some method of support usually in the form of 'intervention'. The details for the *cereal market* are as follows:

| **Imports to EEC** | **Cereals grown in EEC** |
|---|---|
| Target price | Target price |
| Transport charge | |
| Threshold price | |
| Import levy | Market price range |
| (protects EEC from | Intervention price |
| cheaper imports) | |
| Average world | |
| market price | |

**Imports**

*Target price:*
decided annually: represents the level at which it is hoped the market will operate

*Transport charge:*
theoretical cost of moving grain from community port to inland market.

*Threshold price import levy:*
minimum import price difference between world market price and threshold price.

**Internal**

*Market price:*
will depend on day-to-day demand. If it falls too low, grain can be sold into:

*Intervention:*
in practice this means delivery to an official 'intervention store'. There are volume and quality controls to be observed.

## THE FUTURE

### CAP Reform

A recent report from the Commission suggests several possible measures to help reduce budget expenditure:

World prices are normally well below EEC prices. Exports of EEC surpluses are therefore assisted by a subsidy to cover the difference in price levels. Reduction of the gap between levels would reduce EEC expenditure.

Income is provided to the EEC by a charge on imports. However, the EEC is a major exporter and a reduction in the price differentials would provide a *net benefit* to the EEC budget.

Production levels are to be considered again alongside the community requirements. Extended co-responsibility levies could be introduced in an attempt to reduce
production of products in surplus.

Individual member states' contributions will again be re-examined particularly
with the new applicant states to be considered.

Also there is a long-standing policy to remove 'green' currencies altogether which
means some farmers taking price-cuts. The policy will of course be difficult to apply.

## The New Applicant States

Spain and Portugal have requested accession to the Community and their target
date for entry is 1 January 1984. This will mean a greater production of Mediterranean products within the community and also the problem of both Spain and
Portugal's low productivity in comparison with the EEC 10.

The commodities concerned include wine, olive oil, fruit and vegetables, all of
which tend to be labour intensive and already in production in the Mediterranean
regions of existing member states – France, Italy and the new member state, Greece.

Negotiations continue between the new applicants and the EEC 10.

## Greece – the tenth member

As mentioned earlier, Greece joined in 1981. It is worth stating a few figures to
outline the very different agricultural structure of Greece as compared with the
other EEC members:

|  | Greece | EEC9 |
| --- | --- | --- |
| Population | 9m | 260m |
| Percentage of labour force in agricultural employment | 29% | 8% |
| Average area per agricultural holding | 9Hectares | 18Hectares |
| Share of livestock products in total agricultural output | 31% | 59% |
| Contribution of agriculture to gross domestic product | 17% | 4% |
| Share of agricultural products and foodstuffs in: |  |  |
| – total imports | 10% | 20% |
| – total exports | 34% | 8% |

Whatever the problems faced within the CAP, surely any form of unity in Europe
is better than none. But that is a purely personal view!

## IN CONCLUSION

We have looked at the general farming scene; some farm enterprises; farm financial planning; assessment of agricultural propositions; sources of finance and return on capital; co-operatives in agriculture; taxation; the EEC; farming terms and data. I sincerely hope this has been of use to you. Good luck on the farm!

Remember it will be the farmers' *technical and management capabilities* that will determine the level of *farm income* and cash flow. These factors will then determine the *ability to borrow* and the *prudent level of 'gearing'* for the farm business.

# Appendices

## APPENDIX 1—GLOSSARY OF TERMS

### Cattle

Lactation Period – 44 weeks
Gestation Period – 40 weeks

Female:

0–6 months – heifer calf
6–15 months – stirk or young heifer
15 months – 1st calving – heifer – in calf
down calving (within 6 weeks of calving)

Male:

0–6 months – bull calf
6 months – slaughter – bullock or steer (i.e. castrated)
Bull Beef – from the rearing and slaughter of non-castrated animals

### Sheep

Gestation Period – 21 weeks

Female:

0–6 months – lamb
6–12 months – ewe lamb – sometimes mated at this stage
12–24 months – shearling, gimmer, teg or theave
24 months onward – ewe

Male:

0 – 6 months – lamb
6 – 12 months – ram lamb
12 months onwards – ram or tub (i.e. not castrated)
12 months – wether (i.e. castrated)

## Pigs

Gestation Period – 16 weeks

0–8 weeks – suckling pig, or piglet
8–12 weeks – a weaner (i.e. weaned from the sow)
about 22 weeks – a porker
about 26 weeks – a cutter
about 28 weeks – a baconer
about 31 weeks – a heavy hog
6–12 months – a gilt – female for breeding
12 months onward – a sow or a boar

A small weak piglet – a runt or wreckling

## Poultry

0–7 days – chicken
1 week – 18 weeks – pullet (female for egg production)
18 weeks – 21 weeks – point-of-lay pullet
21 weeks onward – hen or cock

1 week – 8 weeks – broiler (meat production)
1 week – 14 weeks – capon (meat production – males implanted with hormone pellet to give a castration effect)

## Turkey

0–7 days – poult
1 week – 12 weeks – mini turkey   hen – female
1 week – 16 weeks – teenage turkey stag – male
1 week – 24 weeks – large turkey

## Production Systems

Battery – system whereby poulty are kept in tiers of cages.
Deep Litter – system whereby poultry are kept under cover on bedding of wood shavings etc.
Free Range – system whereby poultry are allowed to run free.

## General Livestock Terms

Gestation – Length of pregnancy
Lactation – Length of time cow is giving milk
Barren – female no longer capable of breeding
Infertile – male no longer capable of breeding
Cast, Geld or Cull – stock sold for slaughter at the end of its productive life.
    N.B. a cast sheep can mean one which has rolled onto its back and died.
Hermaphrodite or moth – an animal exhibiting both male and female characteristics.
Ruminant – an animal with 4 stomachs, the first of which is called the rumen, i.e. cattle, sheep and goats.

Crossbred – derived by mating two pure breeds.
*or*
Half-bred – if a male of the original pure breed is then used on successive generations we move from ½ bred to ¾ bred, to ⅞ths to ¹⁵⁄₁₆ths. The latter generally being regarded as a pure bred animal.

Pedigree – an animal of a pure breed of known parentage which has been registered with the appropriate breed society.

## Milk Quality

Farm Bottled – straight from the cow to the bottle, having only been filtered and cooled.

Pasteurised – heat treated to kill bacteria.

Sterilised – boiled to kill all germs and increase shelf life.

UHT – ultra high temperature treated to increase shelf life – tastes better than sterilised milk.

Homogenised – treated so that the cream does not settle out.

Butter-fat % – 3.5% legal minimum.

Solids Not Fat (SNF%) – 8.5% legal minimum are paid on a sliding scale relating to these two measurements.

Mastitis – Inflation of the udder caused by bacterial infection – costs the dairy industry £m's each year through lost production.

Raddle – a device fitting to rams which marks ewes during mating thereby assisting flock control.

Ark – a small outdoor pig or poultry house.

## Cropping Terms

Tilth – state of the soil after cultivation and prior to sowing (drilling) seeds, (i.e. good tilth or poor tilth).

Minimal Cultivations – systems of growing crops (usually cereals or kale) whereby ploughing is abandoned in favour of spraying to kill weeds, followed by a sod-seeder, or rotary drill which sows the seeds into silts in the ground.

Corn – often used to cover all cereal varieties in general – but more correctly used an an alternative name for maize.

Forage Crops – grass/kale/turnips or any green crop used for feeding animals either by direct grazing or after harvest and a period of storage (i.e. hay/silage).

Hay – grass conserved for winter feed by drying – either in the field (field cured), or in the barn (barn dried hay).

Oilseed rape – a useful crop grown as a break crop in cropping rotations. Handled by the same basic machinery as cereals, it has a low labour requirement. The black seeds from this yellow-flowering crop produce an edible oil used mainly in the manufacture of margarine and cooking oils. Usually grown on contract for a manufacturer.

Silage – green crops conserved for winter feed by ensiling (acidic fermentation in the absence of air) either in clamps or towers.

# APPENDIX 2—METRICATION

Example: 5 inches = 12.70 centimetres; 5 centimetres = 1.97 inches

| Inches | | Centi-metres | Feet | | Metres | Miles | | Kilo-metres | Fahren-heit | | Centi-grade |
|---|---|---|---|---|---|---|---|---|---|---|---|
| 0.39 | 1 | 2.54 | 3.28 | 1 | 0.30 | 0.62 | 1 | 1.61 | 50 | 10 | −12 |
| 0.79 | 2 | 5.08 | 6.56 | 2 | 0.61 | 1.24 | 2 | 3.22 | 68 | 20 | −7 |
| 1.18 | 3 | 7.62 | 9.84 | 3 | 0.91 | 1.86 | 3 | 4.83 | 86 | 30 | −1 |
| 1.57 | 4 | 10.16 | 13.12 | 4 | 1.22 | 2.49 | 4 | 6.44 | 104 | 40 | 4 |
| 1.97 | 5 | 12.70 | 16.40 | 5 | 1.52 | 3.11 | 5 | 8.05 | 122 | 50 | 10 |
| 2.36 | 6 | 15.24 | 19.69 | 6 | 1.83 | 3.73 | 6 | 9.66 | 140 | 60 | 16 |
| 2.76 | 7 | 17.78 | 22.97 | 7 | 2.13 | 4.35 | 7 | 11.27 | 158 | 70 | 21 |
| 3.15 | 8 | 20.32 | 26.25 | 8 | 2.44 | 4.97 | 8 | 12.87 | 176 | 80 | 27 |
| 3.54 | 9 | 22.86 | 29.53 | 9 | 2.74 | 5.99 | 9 | 14.48 | 194 | 90 | 32 |

| Pints | | Litres | Galls. | | Litres | Ounces | | Gmms. | Pounds | | Kilo-gmms. |
|---|---|---|---|---|---|---|---|---|---|---|---|
| 1.76 | 1 | 0.57 | 0.22 | 1 | 4.55 | 0.04 | 1 | 28.35 | 2.20 | 1 | 0.45 |
| 3.52 | 2 | 1.14 | 0.44 | 2 | 9.09 | 0.07 | 2 | 56.70 | 4.41 | 2 | 0.91 |
| 5.28 | 3 | 1.70 | 0.66 | 3 | 13.64 | 0.11 | 3 | 85.05 | 6.61 | 3 | 1.36 |
| 7.04 | 4 | 2.27 | 0.88 | 4 | 18.18 | 0.14 | 4 | 113.40 | 8.82 | 4 | 1.81 |
| 8.80 | 5 | 2.84 | 1.10 | 5 | 22.73 | 0.18 | 5 | 141.75 | 11.02 | 5 | 2.27 |
| 10.56 | 6 | 3.41 | 1.32 | 6 | 27.28 | 0.21 | 6 | 170.10 | 13.23 | 6 | 2.72 |
| 12.32 | 7 | 3.98 | 1.54 | 7 | 31.82 | 0.25 | 7 | 198.45 | 15.43 | 7 | 3.18 |
| 14.08 | 8 | 4.55 | 1.76 | 8 | 36.37 | 0.28 | 8 | 226.80 | 17.64 | 8 | 3.63 |
| 15.84 | 9 | 5.11 | 1.98 | 9 | 40.91 | 0.32 | 9 | 255.15 | 19.84 | 9 | 4.08 |

| Acres | | Hectares | Tons | | Tonnes | Cwts. per Acre | Kg. per Hectare | Tons per Acre | | Tonnes per Hectare |
|---|---|---|---|---|---|---|---|---|---|---|
| 2.47 | 1 | 0.40 | 0.98 | 1 | 1.02 | 1 | 125.5 | 0.40 | 1 | 2.51 |
| 4.94 | 2 | 0.81 | 1.97 | 2 | 2.03 | 2 | 251.0 | 0.80 | 2 | 5.02 |
| 7.41 | 3 | 1.21 | 2.95 | 3 | 3.05 | 3 | 376.6 | 1.19 | 3 | 7.53 |
| 9.88 | 4 | 1.62 | 3.94 | 4 | 4.06 | 4 | 502.2 | 1.59 | 4 | 10.04 |
| 12.36 | 5 | 2.02 | 4.92 | 5 | 5.08 | 5 | 627.7 | 1.99 | 5 | 12.55 |
| 14.83 | 6 | 2.43 | 5.91 | 6 | 6.10 | 6 | 753.0 | 2.39 | 6 | 15.06 |
| 17.30 | 7 | 2.83 | 6.89 | 7 | 7.11 | 7 | 878.8 | 2.79 | 7 | 17.57 |
| 19.77 | 8 | 3.64 | 7.87 | 8 | 8.13 | 8 | 1,004.0 | 3.19 | 8 | 20.09 |
| 22.24 | 9 | 3.64 | 8.86 | 9 | 9.14 | 9 | 1,130.0 | 3.58 | 9 | 22.60 |

# APPENDIX 2 (CONTINUED)

## Handy Conversion Rules

| To convert | Multiply by | To convert | Multiply by |
|---|---|---|---|
| Inches to centimetres | 2.540 | Centimetres to inches | .3937 |
| Yards to metres | .9144 | Metres to yards | 1.094 |
| Miles to kilometres | 1.609 | Kilometres to miles | .6214 |
| Sq. inches to sq. centimetres | 6.452 | Sq. centimetres to sq. inches | .1550 |
| Sq. yards to sq. metres | .8361 | Sq. metres to sq. yards | 1.196 |
| Acres to hectares | .4047 | Hectares to acres | 2.471 |
| Cubic inches to cubic centimetres | 16.39 | Cubic centimetres to cubic inches | .06102 |
| Cubic yards to cubic metres | .7646 | Cubic metres to cubic yards | 1.308 |
| Gallons to litres | 4.546 | Litres to gallons | .22 |
| Ounces to grammes | 28.35 | Grammes to ounces | .03527 |
| Pounds to kilogrammes | .4536 | Kilogrammes to pounds | 2.205 |
| Tons to kilogrammes | 1016 | Kilogrammes to tons | .0009842 |
| £/score to pence/kilogramme | .0907 | Pence/kilogramme to £/score | 11.025 |
| £/cwt to pence/kilogramme | 1.968 | Pence/kilogramme to £/cwt | .508 |

## Useful Approximations

| | | | | | |
|---|---|---|---|---|---|
| 1 inch | just over | 2½ cm | 1 cwt | just under | 51 kg |
| 1 foot | just under | 30½ cm | 1 gall | just over | 4½ l |
| 1 yard | just under | 91½ cm | 10 lb/gall | just under | 1 kg/l |
| 1 acre | just over | 0.4 ha | 1 cwt/acre | just over | 125 kg/ha |
| 10 lb | just over | 4½ kg | 1 gall/acre | just under | 11¼l/ha |
| 1 score | just over | 9 kg | | | |

## APPENDIX 3—CHECK LIST FOR PRODUCTION STANDARDS AND GROSS MARGIN LEVELS FOR MAIN ENTERPRISES

(Data reference – John Nix, *Farm Management Pocket Book*, Wye College (University of London), 1982.

### Production Level

| | Low | Average | High |
|---|---|---|---|
| (a) = tonnes per hectare (cwt. per acre), unless otherwise specified | | | |
| (b) = £ per hectare (acre) | | | |

**Winter Wheat**
| | Low | Average | High |
|---|---|---|---|
| (a) Yield | 4.25 (34) | 5.25 (42) | 6.25 (50) |
| (b) Gross Margin | 315 (128) | 430 (173) | 540 (218) |

**Spring Wheat**
| | Low | Average | High |
|---|---|---|---|
| (a) Yield | 3.4 (27) | 4.0 (32) | 4.6 (36.5) |
| (b) Gross Margin | 245 (99) | 315 (126) | 380 (153) |

**Spring Barley**
| | Low | Average | High |
|---|---|---|---|
| (a) Yield | 3.5 (28) | 4.1 (32.5) | 4.8 (38) |
| (b) Gross Margin | 258 (104) | 323 (130) | 398 (161) |

**Winter Barley**
| | Low | Average | High |
|---|---|---|---|
| (a) Yield | 4.0 (32) | 4.7 (37.5) | 5.25 (42) |
| (b) Gross Margin | 305 (124) | 380 (154) | 440 (178) |

**Winter Oats**
| | Low | Average | High |
|---|---|---|---|
| (a) Yield | 4.0 (32) | 4.7 (37.5) | 5.25 (42) |
| (b) Gross Margin | 300 (122) | 375 (152) | 430 (175) |

**Spring Oats**
| | Low | Average | High |
|---|---|---|---|
| (a) Yield | 3.5 (28) | 4.1 (32.5) | 4.8 (38) |
| (b) Gross Margin | 250 (101) | 310 (126) | 385 (156) |

**Maincrop Potatoes**
| | Low | Average | High |
|---|---|---|---|
| (a) Yield (tons per acre) | 20 (8) | 30 (12) | 40 (16) |
| (b) Gross Margin | 230 (94) | 770 (311) | 1305 (529) |

**Winter Oil Seed Rape**
| | Low | Average | High |
|---|---|---|---|
| (a) Yield | 1.8 (14.5) | 2.4 (19) | 3.0 (24) |
| (b) Gross Margin | 240 (97) | 375 (152) | 515 (208) |

**Spring Oil Seed Rape**
| | Low | Average | High |
|---|---|---|---|
| (a) Yield | 1.5 (12) | 2.0 (16) | 2.5 (20) |
| (b) Gross Margin | 150 (62) | 265 (107) | 375 (153) |

**Winter Field Beans**
| | Low | Average | High |
|---|---|---|---|
| (a) Yield | 2.25 (18) | 3.0 (24) | 3.75 (30) |
| (b) Gross Margin | 210 (85) | 315 (128) | 420 (170) |

Spring Field Beans
    (a) Yield                      2.0 (16)        2.75 (22)      3.5 (28)
    (b) Gross Margin           190 (77)        300 (121)     405 (165)

## Dairy Cows

A Friesians

| | | | |
|---|---|---|---|
| (a) Yield-litres (gals) | 4,250 (935) | 5,000 (1,100) | 5,750 (1,265) |
| (b) Gross Margin per cow | £286 | £332 | £373 |

B Channel Island Breeds

| | | | |
|---|---|---|---|
| (a) Yield – litres (gals.) | 3,100 (681) | 3,600 (791) | 4,100 (901) |
| (b) Gross Margin per cow | £192 | £229 | £262 |

C Other Breeds (inc. Ayrshires)

| | | | |
|---|---|---|---|
| (a) Yield – litres (gals.) | 3,750 (824) | 4,250 (934) | 4,750 (1,044) |
| (b) Gross Margin per cow | £220 | £249 | £275 |

## Dairy Followers – (Replacements)

A Friesians

| | | | |
|---|---|---|---|
| (a) Total variable costs | £190 | £170 | £150 |
| (b) Gross Margin per heifer | 160 | 165 | 175 |

B Channel Island Breeds

| | | | |
|---|---|---|---|
| (a) Variable costs | £157 | £142 | £127 |
| (b) Gross Margin per heifer | 74 | 74 | 84 |

C Other Breeds

| | | | |
|---|---|---|---|
| (a) Variable Costs | £175 | £160 | £145 |
| (b) Gross Margin per heifer | 107 | 117 | 122 |

## Sheep

| | | | |
|---|---|---|---|
| (a) Lambs reared per ewe | 1.2 | 1.35 | 1.6 |
| (b) Gross Margin per ewe | £17 | £23 | £37 |

## Pigs*

1. *Breeding* (weaners to 25 kg liveweight)
  Breeding sows selling weaners:

| | Average | High |
|---|---|---|
| (a) Weaners sold per sow, per annum | 18 | 22.5 |
| (b) Gross Margin per sow | £95 | £185 |

2. *Fattening* (from 25 kg. liveweight)
  to:

| | Pork | Cutter | Bacon | Heavy |
|---|---|---|---|---|
| Liveweight (kg) | 65 | 82 | 90 | 117 |
| Average Gross Margin per pig | £1.60 | £2.85 | £4.80 | £2.25 |
| Good Gross Margin per pig | £4.90 | £6.30 | £8.85 | £7.05 |

*Note:* Pig results can be *extremely variable* due to prices, mortality rates and food conversion ratios.

## Beef*

1. *Early Weaning* – Bucket rearing (per calf)
   Calf sold at 6 months:
   (a) Variable costs           £76
   (b) Gross Margin per calf    £34

2. *Single Suckling* (per cow)

   |  | Average | High |
   |---|---|---|
   | Late winter/spring calving | | |
   | Gross Margin per cow | £100 | £104 |
   | Autumn/Early Winter calving | | |
   | Gross Margin per cow | £117 | £129 |

3. *Fattening Store Cattle*
   Summer fattening – Gross Margin per Head: £44
   Winter fattening – Gross Margin per Head: £36

4. *18 Month Beef*
   Autumn born calf – Gross Margin per Head: £113
   Spring born calf – Gross Margin per Head: £110

5. *24 Month Beef*
   Autumn born calf – Gross Margin per Head: £102
   Spring born calf – Gross Margin per Head: £120

---

*Beef margins are notoriously difficult to pinpoint – you often find the farmer selling at different stages of livestock-finishing, due to cash flow pressures.

**APPENDIX 4**—FARM VISIT *Aide Memoire*

The following notes may be useful when carrying out a farm visit:

---

Date  . . . . . . .

Farmers' name and address:

Farm Size: . . . . . . . . . . . acres
      (Owned . . . . . . . . . . . . . . . .        rented  . . . . . . . .)
      Rent per annum £  . . . . . .
      Land Grading  . . . . . . . .

Management Structure:

Farm enterprises:                Cereals/dairy/beef/sheep/pigs

Stocking & Cropping plan for the farm:

    Crops:

    Livestock:

    Grass:

Labour availability:
        . . . . . . . full-time men
        . . . . . . . casual

Machinery/Buildings: are they adequate for the stocking and cropping plan?

Financial Data:      available ✔     not available ✗

   (i) Balance sheet and accounts
  (ii) Enterprise recordings
 (iii) Gross margin budget
 (iv) Farmers Balance Sheet
  (v) Cash Flow forecast
 (vi) Bank statements.

Level of funding:

   (i) Overdraft £ . . . . . .
  (ii) Loan £ . . . . . . . . .
 (iii) Any other finance £ . . .

The proposed funding and purpose:

(working capital/farm improvement/farm purchase)

    (i) Overdraft £ . . . . . .
    (ii) Loan £ . . . . . . . . .
    (iii) Other finance £ . . . . . .

Gearing Level:

| | | |
|---|---|---|
| Total assets | £ . . . . . . . . . . | (£ . . . . . . per acre) |
| Net Worth | £ . . . . . . . . . . | Ratio . . . . . :1 |
| Total Debts | £ . . . . . . . . . . | |

Serviceability:

– check           satisfactory ✔      unstatisfactory ✗
    (i) Rental equivalent
    (ii) as a percentage of gross output
    (iii) gross margin budget
    (iv) cash flow forecast
    (v) audited accounts (P & L account)
    (vi) bank statement trends

Security:


Summary:

– comment on

farmers' management ability:

track record:

the level of finance requested:

repayment ability:

security offered:

## APPENDIX 5—SPECIMEN AUDITED ACCOUNTS AND STATISTICS*

Specimen Farmer's

## PROFIT AND LOSS ACCOUNT

Year ended 30th September 1981

|  | 1981 | | 1980 | |
|---|---|---|---|---|
|  | £ | £ | £ | £ |
| GROSS MARGINS – Livestock |  | 56,344 |  | 0 |
| Arable |  | 6,135 |  | 0 |
| TOTAL GROSS MARGINS |  | 62,479 |  | 0 |
| Sundry Receipts |  | 972 |  | 0 |
| GROSS PROFIT |  | 63,451 |  | 0 |
| deduct FIXED COSTS |  |  |  |  |
| Wages | 14,988 |  | 0 |  |
| Power & Machinery | 15,940 |  | 0 |  |
| Rent & Property | 11,444 |  | 0 |  |
| Administration | 1,795 |  | 0 |  |
| Finance | 3,975 |  | 0 |  |
|  |  | 48,142 |  | 0 |
| Management Income |  | 15,309 |  | 0 |
| Adjustment – unrealised profit |  | −475 |  | 0 |
| Financial Profit |  | £14,834 | £ | 0 |

*This specimen farmer's profit and loss account, balance sheet and schedule of farm statistics illustrates a specialised accounting format developed for farmers using a gross margin system.

(Reproduced by courtesy of Thornton Baker, Chartered Accountants.)

**APPENDIX 5** (continued)

Specimen Farmers

BALANCE SHEET

Year ended 30th September 1981

|  | 1981 | | 1980 | |
| --- | --- | --- | --- | --- |
|  | £ | £ | £ | £ |
| ASSETS |  |  |  |  |
| Fixed Assets |  | 48,389 |  | 0 |
| Long-Term Assets |  |  |  |  |
| Dairy Herd |  | 57,650 |  | 0 |
| Breeding Pig Herd |  | 9,845 |  | 0 |
|  |  | 115,884 |  | 0 |
| Current Assets |  |  |  |  |
| Valuation | 50,586 |  | 0 |  |
| Debtors & Payments in Advance | 12,568 |  | 0 |  |
| Cash at Bank | 0 |  | 0 |  |
|  | £63,154 |  | £   0 |  |
| Current Liabilities |  |  |  |  |
| Creditors | 5,614 |  | 0 |  |
| Bank Overdraft | 5,716 |  | 0 |  |
| Bank Loan | 11,600 |  | 0 |  |
| Private Loan | 1,000 |  | 0 |  |
|  | £23930 |  | £   0 |  |
| Net Current Assets |  | 39,224 |  | 0 |
| NET ASSETS |  | £155,108 |  | £   0 |
| Financed by |  |  |  |  |
| Capital Accounts |  | 155,108 |  | 0 |
| CAPITAL EMPLOYED |  | £155,108 |  | £   0 |

**APPENDIX 5**—(continued)

Specimen Farmers

FARM STATISTICS

Year ended 30th September 1981

|  | 1981 |
|---|---|
| Total Livestock in Acres | 247 |
| Total Arable in Acres | 272 |
| Total Farm in Acres | 519 |
| Livestock Margin per Acre | 228.11 |
| Arable Margin per Acre | 22.56 |
| Profit per Acre | 28.58 |
| Turnover per Acre | 274.71 |
| Rental Equivalent | |
|     Rent | 8,000 |
|     Interest – Overdraft | 2,325 |
|     Interest – Bank Loan | 1,500 |
| | 11,825 |
| Rental Equivalent per Acre | 22.78 |
| Fixed Costs per Acre | |
|     Wages | 28.88 |
|     Power & Machinery | 30.71 |
|     Rent & Property | 22.05 |
|     Adminstration | 3.46 |
|     Finance | 7.66 |
| | 92.76 |
| Management Income before Finance Charges per Acre | 37.16 |
| Management Income/Gross Capital Employed | 11.12 % |
| External Borrowings/Net Worth | 11.81 % |
| Finance Charges/Turnover | 2.79 % |
| External Borrowings/Turnover | 12.85 % |
| Gross Capital Employed per Acre | 334.15 |

These statistics are included only for the basis of comparison from year to year and should not be compared with published industry figures

## APPENDIX 6—SPECIMEN FORM FOR BANK/BRANCH USE ON REVIEW OF FARMING ACCOUNTS

*Date*                                                    *Branch*

*Customer's name and address*

*Farm size*

       Owned

       Rented

       ———

       Total       (acres)

       ———

*Main farm enterprises*

*Security held*

*Bank account statistics*

    Limit: overdraft

          loan

    Average balance

    Turnover

    Highest balance

    Lowest balance

    % uptake of overdraft

**APPENDIX 6** (continued)

*From Audited Accounts*

|  | date | date |
|---|---|---|
| Year end |  |  |
| Surplus (net worth) |  |  |
| Creditors |  |  |
| Hire purchase |  |  |
| Bank borrowing |  |  |
| Mortgages |  |  |
| Net profit |  |  |

*From Farmer's Balance Sheet.*    Date:

Surplus (net worth)
  Land valuation:

*Tenant's assets* per acre:   £

*Rental equivalent* per acre:   £

*Management accounts available*        Yes/No

Note: By completing a form like this for each of your farming customers, you can build up a comparative picture of the farm businesses in your own area.

## APPENDIX 7—MILK MARKETING BOARD FORWARD BUDGET

| Enterprise | Number | Gross Margin £ | Total £ |
|---|---|---|---|
| DAIRY HERD | 124.7 | 394.7 | 49,226 |
| DAIRY REPLACEMENTS | 199.9 | 25.9 | 5,185 |
| WINTER WHEAT | 78.5 | 408.9* | 32,101 |
| SPRING WHEAT | 4.0 | 217.8* | 871 |
| WINTER BARLEY | 32.8 | 499.6* | 16,388 |
| SPRING BARLEY | 11.3 | 236.5* | 2,672 |
| OIL SEED RAPE | 25.9 | 534.7* | 13,849 |
| Less Forage Costs | | | 12,274 |
| Other receipts | | | 1,770 |
| Adjustment | | | +2,860 |
| INCOME less Variable Costs | | | 112,648 |
| Wages | | | 18,865 |
| Power and machinery | | | 19,738 |
| Sundries | | | 8,739 |
| Property charges | | | 19,101 |
| Bank charges and interest | | | 1,859 |
| Other interest | | | 6,512 |
| TOTAL FIXED COSTS | | | 74,814 |
| PROFIT (Before Depreciation) | | | 37,834 |

*Per hectare.

The Farm Management Services Division of the Milk Marketing Board can help the farmer plan his production and assist him with his book-keeping.

A number of services are offered ranging from milk recording schemes to a full consultancy service covering all the farm enterprises. The consultancy officer will also help with the preparation of cash flow forecasts. The budget above is an example of the MMB's work and illustrates the use of gross margin techniques described earlier in the main text.

Note: The *projected profit figure* should always be compared with past performance of the farm business.

## APPENDIX 8—ADAS GROSS MARGIN ANALYSIS FORM

# ENTERPRISE GROSS MARGINS

### A.   LIVESTOCK - PER HEAD

| CLASS OF STOCK | | | | | |
|---|---|---|---|---|---|
| Number of Livestock | | | | | |
| LIVESTOCK OUTPUT   (a) | | | | | |
| VARIABLE COSTS
Bought and Homegrown Concentrates | | | | | |
| Other Bought Feed | | | | | |
| Veterinary and medicines | | | | | |
| Others | | | | | |
| Sub Total   (b) | | | | | |
| GROSS MARGIN   (a - b)
(excluding forage) | | | | | |
| Bought Concentrates (tonnes) | | | | | |
| Food costs per £100 Output | | | | | |

### B.   FORAGE VARIABLE COSTS per hectare

| TYPE OF CROP | | | |
|---|---|---|---|
| Hectares | | | |
| Fertilizers | | | |
| Seed and Others | | | |
| VARIABLE COSTS | | | |

**TOTAL FORAGE AREA** — HECTARES

**GRAZING LIVESTOCK UNITS PER ADJUSTED FORAGE HECTARE** — G.L.U's

### C.   GRAZING LIVESTOCK

| | Grazing Livestock Units | % of Total Grazing Livestock Units |
|---|---|---|
| DAIRY COWS | | |
| BEEF | | |
| SHEEP | | |
| TOTAL | | 100% |

**GROSS MARGIN PER GRAZING LIVESTOCK UNIT**
(before forage costs) — £

### D.   GROSS MARGIN PER HECTARE FROM FORAGE AREA

£

### E.   DAIRY

| MILK YIELD PER COW   Litres | |
|---|---|
| MILK VALUE PER COW   £ | |
| MARGIN OVER CONCENTRATES
PER COW   £ | |

**CONCENTRATES KG/LITRE** — Kg

(22365)

**APPENDIX 8** (continued)

# ENTERPRISE GROSS MARGINS

**F.   CASH CROPS - PER HECTARE**

CROPS SOWN/PLANTED DURING RECORDING YEAR

| | | | | | | | | |
|---|---|---|---|---|---|---|---|---|
| **CROP YEAR** | | | | | | | | |
| **HECTARES** | | | | | | | | |
| **CROP OUTPUT**    (a) | | | | | | | | |
| **VARIABLE COSTS**<br>Fertilizers | | | | | | | | |
| Seed - Home Grown and Purchased | | | | | | | | |
| Sprays | | | | | | | | |
| Casual Labour and Contract | | | | | | | | |
| Others | | | | | | | | |
| **TOTAL VARIABLE COSTS**     (b) | | | | | | | | |
| **GROSS MARGIN**    (a - b) | | | | | | | | |
| **YIELD**  (Tonnes) | | | | | | | | |

---

**TOTAL CASH CROP HECTARES**

ha

**GROSS MARGIN PER HECTARE FROM CASH CROPS**

£

---

**EFFICIENCY INDICES**

£

GROSS MARGIN PER HECTARE

GROSS MARGIN PER £100 WAGES

GROSS MARGIN PER £100 POWER AND MACHINERY

**APPENDIX 8** (continued)

# FINANCIAL SUMMARY

**GROSS MARGINS**

£

| | |
|---|---|
| CASH CROPS | |
| GRAZING LIVESTOCK | |
| INTENSIVE LIVESTOCK | |
| OTHER RECEIPTS/GRANTS | |
| **TOTAL GROSS MARGIN** | (a) |

**FIXED COSTS**

£

| | |
|---|---|
| WAGES | |
| MANAGEMENT | |
| POWER AND MACHINERY | |
| PROPERTY CHARGES | |
| SUNDRIES | |
| **TOTAL** | (b) |
| **SURPLUS/DEFICIT** | (a - b) = (c) |
| FINANCING CHARGES (d) | |
| **SURPLUS/DEFICIT** (Including Financing Charges) | (c - d) |

**FIXED COSTS - PER HECTARE**

£

| | |
|---|---|
| WAGES | |
| MANAGEMENT | |
| POWER AND MACHINERY | |
| PROPERTY CHARGES | |
| SUNDRIES | |
| FINANCING CHARGES | |
| **TOTAL FIXED COSTS** | |

POWER AND MACHINERY DETAILS

| | |
|---|---|
| Machinery and Vehicle repairs | |
| Fuel and Oil | |
| Contract Hire, Transport | |
| Leasing Charges | |
| Electricity and Coal | |
| Machinery depreciation | |
| Vehicle Tax and Insurance | |
| Others | |

**SURPLUS/DEFICIT (incl FINANCING CHARGES) PER HECTARE**

**ADVISER'S COMMENTS**

Bm 22365/1/5424/141 1m 12/77 TCL/Bf

## APPENDIX 9—MEAT AND LIVESTOCK COMMISSION (MLC)

Financed by the agricultural industry, MLC provides a wide range of costing/consultancy services to farmers, including the preparation of cash flow forecasts and gross margin budgets. The MLC covers all the main livestock sections – i.e. beef, sheep and pigs. The Commission also produces various booklets covering production techniques, farming economics and marketing.

The form opposite is from an MLC booklet on 'Beef Improvement Services'. The objective is to help the farmer to maximise beef profitability by control of costs and land utilisation. The farmer does the basic recording of data which is then processed by MLC staff to produce a final report for discussion.

**MLC**

# BEEFPLAN
## GRASSLAND REPORT

Name.... F. GILES ....... Date completed..... 14 / 11 / 80

GRASSLAND ...................................................

| Area: | Leys | **50** ha |
|---|---|---|
| | Permanent Pasture | **5** ha |
| | Rough grazing | ha |
| | Hill | ha |
| | **TOTAL** | **55** ha |

Grazing season
| | | | |
|---|---|---|---|
| – start | **20** | **04** | |
| – end | **05** | **11** | |
| – no. of days | **197** | | |

**UTILISATION**

| 18-month beef | **17·1** ha |
|---|---|
| Sucklers | **8·8** ha |
| Ewes and Lambs | **7·3** ha |
| Ponies | **0·7** ha |
| | ha |
| | ha |
| | ha |

**CONSERVATION**

Amount made
| Silage | **400** tonnes |
|---|---|
| Hay | **20** tonnes |

Area allocated
| **18·0** ha |
|---|
| **3·1** ha |

| | YOUR RESULT | YOUR TARGET |
|---|---|---|
| | per hectare | per hectare |
| Livestock units | **2·25** | **2·9** |
| Nitrogen | **153** kg | **150** kg |

**VARIABLE COSTS**

| | Total £ | £/ha | £/ha |
|---|---|---|---|
| Fertiliser – Nitrogen and compounds | **4161** | **75·66** | **75** |
| Lime and slag | **100** | **1·82** | **2** |
| Seeds and Sprays | **250** | **4·55** | **5** |
| Other costs | **150** | **2·73** | **3** |
| | | | |
| | | | |
| **TOTAL GRASSLAND COSTS** | **4661** | **84·76** | **85** |
| **FORAGE CROP COSTS** Brought forward | **0** | **0** | **0** |
| **TOTAL FORAGE COSTS** | **4661** | **84·76** | **85** |

MEAT AND LIVESTOCK COMMISSION

## APPENDIX 10—CHECK LIST

**To review farm business finance:**

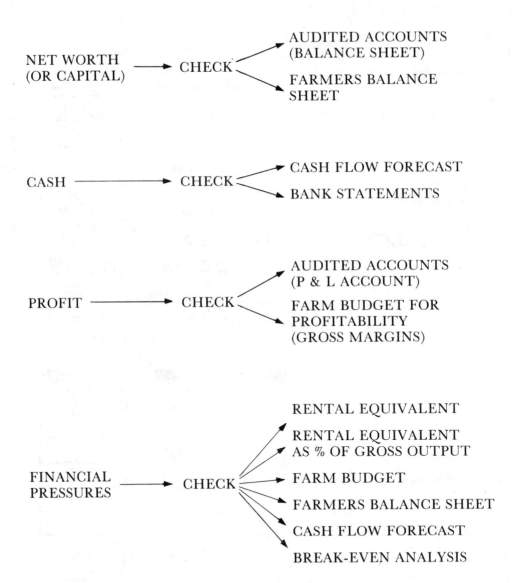

NET WORTH (OR CAPITAL) → CHECK
- AUDITED ACCOUNTS (BALANCE SHEET)
- FARMERS BALANCE SHEET

CASH → CHECK
- CASH FLOW FORECAST
- BANK STATEMENTS

PROFIT → CHECK
- AUDITED ACCOUNTS (P & L ACCOUNT)
- FARM BUDGET FOR PROFITABILITY (GROSS MARGINS)

FINANCIAL PRESSURES → CHECK
- RENTAL EQUIVALENT
- RENTAL EQUIVALENT AS % OF GROSS OUTPUT
- FARM BUDGET
- FARMERS BALANCE SHEET
- CASH FLOW FORECAST
- BREAK-EVEN ANALYSIS

## APPENDIX 11—ADAS FARM DEVELOPMENT PLAN

The following three pages are only a small extract from a set of *guidelines* for a six-year development plan which could be prepared by the ADAS section of the Ministry of Agriculture working in conjunction with the farmer.

The exhibits outline the main points in the plan. In the first two pages the basic objectives, strategy and planned stocking and cropping changes are detailed. The final page is a summary showing the prospective financial performance at the completion of the development plan compared with the start point (the base year normalised – i.e. after adjusting for any extraordinary factors affecting output in that year).

The surplus of £46,630 shows an increase of £26,735 compared with the start year – this looks substantial and the banker should discuss the figures with the farmer. Bank finance will almost certainly be involved notwithstanding the Ministry grant.

N.B. The Farm and Horticulture Development Scheme has been renamed – Agriculture and Horticulture Development Scheme (AHDS).

# APPENDIX 11 (continued)

MINISTRY OF AGRICULTURE FISHERIES AND FOOD

AGRICULTURAL DEVELOPMENT AND ADVISORY SERVICE

FARM AND HORTICULTURE DEVELOPMENT SCHEME

DEVELOPMENT PLAN EXAMPLE

I    OBJECTIVE

The Plan will be of 6 years duration and on completion the budgeted earned income per labour unit will be greater than £4,200 using current financial data.

II    STRATEGY

(a)  Land Improvement

Drain an area of permanent pasture and bring into arable rotation, thus allowing the area of winter wheat to be increased, and an extra area of short term grass leys to boost grassland productivity. Re-seed an area of permanent pasture. The improved grassland output will enable the sheep and cattle numbers to be increased.

(b)  Brussels Sprouts

Increase the brussels sprout area to justify the introduction of mechanical harvesting, so reducing the input of casual labour.

(c)  Hops

Continue replanting to high Alpha varieties to maximize markets returns. Improve hop drying and handling facilities to reduce labour at harvest. Renew hop wire work to allow further mechanisation in the hop garden.

(d)  Dessert Apples

Reduce labour for apple harvesting and storage by the introduction of bulk bins, with the necessary alterations to existing cold stores. Grub and replant as needed to maintain age structure of orchards for optimum production. Extend windbreaks where necessary.

(e)  Sheep

Increase the number of breeding ewes and improve sheep handling facilities to reduce labour input and allow more efficient management of the flock. The extension of grass leys to other parts of the farm will require the provision of some new boundary and internal sheep-proof fences.

(f)  Beef

Retain the single suckled weaned calves and fatten out of yards at about 16-18 months age. Change-over to silage as the main winter feed, which will necessitate building a clamp silo and purchasing a range of silage making machinery. Build new yard for finishing the weaned calves.

## APPENDIX 11 (continued)

III   CROPPING AND STOCKING CHANGES

|  | PRESENT | YEAR 6 |
|---|---|---|
| Winter Wheat | 12.1 ha | 40.5 ha |
| Barley | 48.6 | 20.2 |
| Brussels Sprouts | 4.8 | 10.1 |
| Hops | 17.0 | 17.0 |
| Apples - Dessert | 38.5 | 38.5 |
| Grass | 60.0 | 54.7 |
|  | 181.0 ha | 181.0 ha |
| Suckler Cows | 40 | 40 |
| Fat Cattle | - | 38 |
| Breeding Ewes | 200 | 300 |

IV   LABOUR

|  | PRESENT | YEAR 6 |
|---|---|---|
| Regular | 26,764 hours | 24,464 hours |
| Casual | 16,842 | 16,480 |
| Occupier | 2,000 | 2,000 |
|  | 45,606 hours | 42,944 hours |
| Labour Units | 20.7 | 19.5 |

(1 unit = 2,200 hours)

## APPENDIX 11 (continued)

MINISTRY OF AGRICULTURE FISHERIES AND FOOD
AGRICULTURAL DEVELOPMENT AND ADVISORY SERVICE          FM NO. _____

**Budgeting form**                                    OCCUPANCY OF HOLDING

### WHOLE FARM TRADING SUMMARY

| | Hectares |
|---|---|
| Owner-occupied _____ | 181 |
| Rented on Secure Tenancy _____ | |
| Other Land Farmed _____ | |
| TOTAL AREA _____ | 181 |

| | | BASE YEAR NORMALISED | FINAL YEAR |
|---|---|---|---|
| | | £ | £ |
| **ENTERPRISE GROSS MARGINS** | WHEAT | 3566 | 11935 |
| | BARLEY | 10974 | 5026 |
| | APPLES | 69030 | 80657 |
| | BRUSSELS SPROUTS | 7115 | 16480 |
| | HOPS | 26945 | 33405 |
| | BEEF | 4796 | 7116 |
| | SHEEP | 4792 | 7149 |
| | | | |
| | | | |
| **GROSS MARGIN** (before forage costs) | | 127218 | 161768 |
| FORAGE VARIABLE COSTS | | 2027 | 2943 |
| **GROSS MARGIN** (after forage costs) | | 125191 | 158825 |
| SUNDRY RECEIPTS | | | |
| TOTAL | | 125191 | 158825 |
| **FIXED COSTS** (before financing charges) | | 98131 | 104335 |
| **SURPLUS/DEFICIT** (before financing charges) | | 27060 | 54490 |
| Financing Charges | | 7165 | 7860 |
| **SURPLUS/DEFICIT** (after financing charges) | | 19895 | 46630 |

**FD 2/14**

## APPENDIX 12—USEFUL ADDRESSES

AGRICULTURAL CREDIT CORPORATION LTD:
Agriculture House, 25–31 Knightsbridge, London SW1X 7NJ. (Tel: 01-235 6296).

AGRICULTURAL DEVELOPMENT AND ADVISORY SERVICE:
Great Westminster House, Horseferry Road, London SW1P 2AE. (Tel: 01-216 6311).

AGRICULTURAL MORTGAGE CORPORATION LTD:
Bucklersbury House, 3 Queen Victoria Street, London EC4N 8DU. (Tel: 01-236 5252)

AGRICULTURAL TRAINING BOARD:
Bourne House, 32–34 Beckenham Road, Beckenham, Kent BR3 4PB. (Tel: 01-650 4890).

BRITISH AGRICULTURAL EXPORT COUNCIL:
35 Belgrave Square, London SW1X 8QN. (Tel: 01-245 9819).

BRITISH WOOL MARKETING BOARD:
Oak Mills, Station Road, Clayton, Bradford, W. Yorkshire BD14 6JD. (Tel: 0274 882091).

CENTRAL COUNCIL FOR AGRICULTURAL AND HORTICULTURAL CO-OPERATION:
301–344 Market Towers, New Convent Garden Market, 1 Nine Elms Lane, London SW8 5NQ. (Tel: 01-720 2144).

COUNTRYSIDE COMMISSION:
John Dower House, Crescent Place, Cheltenham, Gloucestershire GL50 3RA. (Tel: 0242 21381).

DEPARTMENT OF AGRICULTURE AND FISHERIES FOR SCOTLAND:
Chesser House, 500 Gorgie Road, Edinburgh EH11 3AW. (Tel: 031-443 4020).

EUROPEAN COMMUNITY INFORMATION OFFICE:
20 Kensington Palace Gardens, London W8 4QQ. (Tel: 01-727 8090).

FARMERS UNION OF WALES:
Llys Amaeth, Queen's Square, Aberystwyth, Dyfed SY23 2EA. (Tel: 0970 612755).

FORESTRY COMMISSION:
231 Corstorphine Road, Edinburgh EH12 7AT. (Tel: 031-334 0303).

HER MAJESTY'S STATIONERY OFFICE (ORDERS):
P.O. Box 569, 49 High Holborn, London WC1V 6HB. (Tel: 01-928 1321).

HOME GROWN CEREALS AUTHORITY:
Hamlyn House, Highgate Hill, London N19 5PR. (Tel: 01-263 3391).

INSTITUTE OF AGRICULTURAL SECRETARIES:
N.A.C. Stoneleigh, Kenilworth, Warwickshire CV8 2LZ. (Tel: 0203 20623).

LAND SETTLEMENT ASSOCIATION LTD:
43 Cromwell Road, London SW7 2EE. (Tel: 01-589 9066).

MEAT AND LIVESTOCK COMMISSION:
P.O. Box 44. Queensway House, Bletchley, Milton Keynes MK2 2EF. (Tel: 0908 74941).

MILK MARKETING BOARD:
Thames Ditton, Surrey KT7 0EL. (Tel: 01-398 4101).

MINISTRY OF AGRICULTURE, FISHERIES AND FOOD:
Whitehall Place, London SW1A 2HH. (Tel: 01-233 3000).

NATIONAL AGRICULTURAL CENTRE:
Stoneleigh, Kenilworth CV8 2LZ. (Tel: 0203 56151).

NATIONAL FARMERS UNION:
Agriculture House, 25–31 Knightsbridge, London SW1X 7NJ. (Tel: 01-235 5077).

NATIONAL FEDERATION OF YOUNG FARMERS CLUBS:
Y.F.C. Centre, N.A.C., Kenilworth CV8 2LG. (Tel: 0203 56131).

SCOTTISH AGRICULTURAL ORGANISATION SOCIETY LTD:
18–19 Claremont Crescent, Edinburgh EH7 4JW. (Tel: 031-556 6574).

WELSH AGRICULTURAL ORGANISATION SOCIETY LTD:
Brynawel, P.O. 8, Aberystwyth, Dyfed SY23 1DR. (Tel: 0970 4011).

# Index

Addresses, useful .................................................. 140
Agriculture in the national economy ........................... 2, 5, 67
    Annual Review of ........................................... 1
    Agricultural Credit Corporation (ACC) .......................... 72
    Development and Advisory Service (ADAS): farm development plan .. 136
    and Horticultural Development Scheme (AHDS) ................. 78
        Grant Scheme (AHGS) ................................. 78
    Mortgage Corporation (AMC) ............................... 74
'Agristats' ........................................................ 5
Asset cover ....................................................... 38
Audited accounts ............................................. 38, 39

Balance sheets ........................ 33, 38, 40 et seq., 51 et seq., 124
Bank finance .................................. 2, 10, 37 et seq., 89
    application for sanction .......................................... 65
    security for .................................................... 64
    servicing the borrowing ......................................... 46
Barley ............................................................ 21
Beef production .......................................... 15, 119
Break-even analysis ............................................... 59
Budgets .................................... 29, 30, 38, 48

Capital ....................................................... 8, 79
    expenditure allowance ......................................... 100
    gains tax ..................................................... 100
    return on, .................................................... 79
    transfer tax .................................................. 100
Cash flow .............................................. 37, 60 et seq.
Cattle ................................................... 8, 13, 15
    return on capital ............................................. 81

Cereals . . . . . . . . . . . . . . . . . . . . . . . . . . . . . . . . . . . . . . . . . . . . . . . . . . . . . . . . . .   21
    return on capital . . . . . . . . . . . . . . . . . . . . . . . . . . . . . . . . . . . . . . . . . .   82, 118
Common Agricultural Policy (CAP) . . . . . . . . . . . . . . . . . . . . . . . . . . .   105, 109
    Market . . . . . . . . . . . . . . . . . . . . . . . . . . . . . . . . . . . . . . . . . . . . . . . . .   103 et seq.
Cooperatives in agriculture . . . . . . . . . . . . . . . . . . . . . . . . . . . . . . . . . . .   85 et seq.

Dairy production . . . . . . . . . . . . . . . . . . . . . . . . . . . . . . . . . . . . . . . . . . .   13, 119
    return on capital . . . . . . . . . . . . . . . . . . . . . . . . . . . . . . . . . . . . . . . . .   81

Enterprise monitoring . . . . . . . . . . . . . . . . . . . . . . . . . . . . . . . . . . . . . . .   15
European Economic Community . . . . . . . . . . . . . . . . . . . . . . . . . . . . .   103 et seq.

Farm incomes . . . . . . . . . . . . . . . . . . . . . . . . . . . . . . . . . . . . . . . . . . . . . .   28
    size . . . . . . . . . . . . . . . . . . . . . . . . . . . . . . . . . . . . . . . . . . . . . . . . . . . .   1, 7
    statistics . . . . . . . . . . . . . . . . . . . . . . . . . . . . . . . . . . . . . . . . . . . . . . .   125
    types . . . . . . . . . . . . . . . . . . . . . . . . . . . . . . . . . . . . . . . . . . . . . . . . . .   3
    visits . . . . . . . . . . . . . . . . . . . . . . . . . . . . . . . . . . . . . . . . . . . . . . . . . .   38, 121
Farms, decline in number . . . . . . . . . . . . . . . . . . . . . . . . . . . . . . . . . . .   2
Finance, sources of . . . . . . . . . . . . . . . . . . . . . . . . . . . . . . . . . . . . . . . . .   67 et seq.
Financial performance . . . . . . . . . . . . . . . . . . . . . . . . . . . . . . . . . . . . . .   38
    planning . . . . . . . . . . . . . . . . . . . . . . . . . . . . . . . . . . . . . . . . .   25 et seq., 37
'Flying herd' . . . . . . . . . . . . . . . . . . . . . . . . . . . . . . . . . . . . . . . . . . . . . .   15
Forage crops . . . . . . . . . . . . . . . . . . . . . . . . . . . . . . . . . . . . . . . . . . . . . . .   115
Foreign currency loans . . . . . . . . . . . . . . . . . . . . . . . . . . . . . . . . . . . . . .   78

Gearing . . . . . . . . . . . . . . . . . . . . . . . . . . . . . . . . . . . . . . . . . . . . . . . . . . .   45
Glossary . . . . . . . . . . . . . . . . . . . . . . . . . . . . . . . . . . . . . . . . . . . . . . . . . .   113 et seq.
Grants, government . . . . . . . . . . . . . . . . . . . . . . . . . . . . . . . . . . . . . . . . .   77
Grass, dried . . . . . . . . . . . . . . . . . . . . . . . . . . . . . . . . . . . . . . . . . . . . . . .   22
Grassland production . . . . . . . . . . . . . . . . . . . . . . . . . . . . . . . . . . . . . . .   22
Grazing systems . . . . . . . . . . . . . . . . . . . . . . . . . . . . . . . . . . . . . . . . . . .   23, 115
Green money . . . . . . . . . . . . . . . . . . . . . . . . . . . . . . . . . . . . . . . . . . . . . .   107
Gross margin . . . . . . . . . . . . . . . . . . . . . . . . . . . . . . . . . .   25 et seq., 49, 55, 129

Hay . . . . . . . . . . . . . . . . . . . . . . . . . . . . . . . . . . . . . . . . . . . . . . . . . . . . . . .   22
Herd basis . . . . . . . . . . . . . . . . . . . . . . . . . . . . . . . . . . . . . . . . . . . . . . . . .   99
Hire purchase . . . . . . . . . . . . . . . . . . . . . . . . . . . . . . . . . . . . . . . . . . . . . .   70

Income . . . . . . . . . . . . . . . . . . . . . . . . . . . . . . . . . . . . . . . . . . . . . . . . . . . .   2, 8
    tax . . . . . . . . . . . . . . . . . . . . . . . . . . . . . . . . . . . . . . . . . . . . . . . . . . . . .   99
Insurance companies, mortgages from . . . . . . . . . . . . . . . . . . . . . . . . . .   72

Land, classification ........................................................... 3

    prices ................................................................ 2, 9

    tenure ................................................................. 9

    usage .................................................................. 2, 5

Leasing ................................................................ 69, 70, 90

Livestock, numbers ........................................................ 2, 6

    terms ................................................................. 104

Loans, private ............................................................ 72

    foreign currency ...................................................... 79

    (see also Bank finance)

Lowland sheep production ...................................................... 18


Management control and monitoring .......................................... 29

Meat and Livestock Commission (MLC) ........................................ 132

Metrication .............................................................. 116

Milk ................................................................. 13, ,81, 115

    Marketing Board budget ................................................ 128

Minimal cultivations ........................................................ 115


Net worth ............................................................. 31, 45


Oats .................................................................. 21

Output ................................................................. 8


Pig production .......................................................... 18, 114, 119

    return on capital ..................................................... 83

Point of Sale credit ......................................................... 68

Poultry .............................................................. 114

Production yields in 1981 .................................................... 2, 7

Profit and Loss account ...................................................... 123

    averaging ............................................................. 99

Profitability budget ......................................................... 29, 30


Rents and rentals ........................................................... 2, 9, 46, 47

Return on capital ........................................................... 79


Sale and leaseback ......................................................... 78

'Serviceability' ........................................................... 46

Sheep production ........................................................... 17, 113

    return on capital ..................................................... 81, 119

Silage . . . . . . . . . . . . . . . . . . . . . . . . . . . . . . . . . . . . . . . . . . . .   22, 115
Stock relief . . . . . . . . . . . . . . . . . . . . . . . . . . . . . . . . . . . . . . . . . .   99
Stocking rate . . . . . . . . . . . . . . . . . . . . . . . . . . . . . . . . . . . . . . . .   15
Syndicate credit . . . . . . . . . . . . . . . . . . . . . . . . . . . . . . . . . . . . . . .   71


Taxation . . . . . . . . . . . . . . . . . . . . . . . . . . . . . . . . . . . . . . . . .   99 et seq.
Trade credits . . . . . . . . . . . . . . . . . . . . . . . . . . . . . . . . . . . . . . . .   68
Turkeys . . . . . . . . . . . . . . . . . . . . . . . . . . . . . . . . . . . . . . . . . .   114


Visiting the farm . . . . . . . . . . . . . . . . . . . . . . . . . . . . . . . . . . . . .   38, 121


Wheat . . . . . . . . . . . . . . . . . . . . . . . . . . . . . . . . . . . . . . . . . . .   21


Zero grazing . . . . . . . . . . . . . . . . . . . . . . . . . . . . . . . . . . . . . . . .   115